Who Rules Britannia?

Philip Bushill-Matthews

© Philip Bushill-Matthews 2005

All rights reserved. No part of this publication may be reproduced or transmitted in any form or by any means, electronic or mechanical, including photocopying, recording, or any information storage and retrieval system, without prior permission in writing from the publisher. The right of Philip Bushill-Matthews to be identified as the author of this work has been asserted by him in accordance with the Copyright, Designs and Patents Act 1988.

ISBN 0 9549137-0-1

Published by
Polperro Heritage Press
Clifton-upon-Teme
Worcestershire WR6 6EN UK
www.polperropress.co.uk

Cover design by David Lock and Steve Bowgen

Printed by Orphans Press
Leominster HR6 8JT

Acknowledgements

Many of my Conservative MEP colleagues have helped me, directly or indirectly, in putting this book together. In thanking all of them, I would just like to single out for special mention fellow West-Midlander Malcolm Harbour who has done more to drive the successful completion of the Single Market than anyone else I know.

I also pay tribute to Jonathan Evans, who has been an inspirational Leader of the Conservative MEPs throughout very challenging times.

To those who have bought the book, those who borrow it, and those in both categories who actually read it, I hope you find it of interest.

The facts come from many sources. Unless stated otherwise, the opinions are my own.

In sharing the facts, I trust that many will end up sharing the opinions as well and will persuade others to vote accordingly in the future. Votes are too precious to be squandered.

P. B-M

To

PHILIP GRETTON

who has asked for it

CONTENTS

	Introduction	7
1	The Price of Protest	9
2	Europe sees Red	14
3	Reigning in Spain	26
4	To EPP or Not To EPP	32
5	The Uncommon Market	44
6	Should Norway be Our Way?	55
7	Christmas Votes for Turkey	64
8	Playing to the Gallery	71
9	An Australian Agenda	75
10	A Disunited Kingdom	79
11	Flemings and Lemmings	83
12	The Voice of America	85
13	A Political Project	89
14	The Glory that was France	95
15	Metric Matters	100
16	Time is on Our Side	106
17	The New Battlegrounds	113
18	Absent Friends	119
19	The Kommissars	123
20	Not Enough Rules	132
21	Counting the Cost	137
22	The Great Deception	140

INTRODUCTION

We British are mighty proud of our country and of its place in history. We are so much better than the Europeans – or so people keep telling me.

We developed the 'V' sign to remind the French that our archers who beat them at Agincourt still had their two fingers ready to fire again. In business we refer to 'Spanish customs' when we describe out-of-date practices that haven't changed in years. And when the Germans beat us at football in the World Cup all those years ago the running joke was that the Germans may have beaten us once at our national sport, but we had beaten them twice at theirs...

We have ruled the largest empire the world has ever known. We have not been invaded successfully for a thousand years. We have our very own Royal Family (its Norman/ House of Orange/Hanoverian forbears long forgotten). We have shown the world the meaning of real Parliamentary democracy. We accept the need for some international rules – as long as we set them. But if God had meant us to be part of Europe he would not have dug the Channel. We don't need Johnny Foreigner to tell us what to do...

I have heard such stirring sentiments far and wide as I have campaigned for election. I have heard our Westminster Parliament praised as the true bastion of democracy – especially by MPs. But I have also heard on the doorsteps the growing conviction that politicians have steadily been giving away our national sovereignty to Brussels, that we no longer make our own laws, and the sooner we did so again the better.

Some have gone so far as to say that they had been lied to by Edward Heath back in the 70's as part of a Great Deception. They thought they had voted for free trade, for a 'Common Market'. They wanted it then, and they still wanted it now.

They believed saying 'No' to the EU in its current form would finally produce it. At the very least, a 'protest vote' against the unelected Brussels Bureaucrats who now apparently rule the UK would cost nothing. It would be bound to help the cause.

They could not have been more wrong on all three counts.

CHAPTER 1

The Price of Protest

The decision to join the EEC, as it was originally called, was made by the UK Government following a vote in favour by MPs in Westminster.

Only MPs had the legal authority to say 'Yes' to go in. Only MPs would have the legal authority to say 'No' and come out. MEPs have no say in the matter at all, except as individual voters in any referendum. That is why it was always absurd to elect UKIP MEPs on a platform of saying 'No' when MEPs could say no such thing. UKIP knew this, but said that this logic was irrelevant.

UKIP knows it can never win a General Election. Its objective in 2004 was to register a protest vote. It claimed that such a vote could have no downside as the European Parliament didn't matter. It claimed the upside was that a strong message would get through to Westminster. Like the rest of UKIP message, this was simply not true. The downside has been immense. The message received in Westminster is not the message intended.

The downside became apparent in the simple election arithmetic. In the 1999 European Parliament elections the Conservatives had topped the poll, with 36 Tory MEPs out of a possible 87 UK seats. Labour had come second with 27 and Liberal Democrats third with ten.

In 2004 the 87 UK seats reduced to 78, as part of a deal to allocate seats to MEPs from the ten new countries joining from Central and Eastern Europe. So there were going to be nine less UK MEPs overall: the question was which party would lose out? Mathematically, based on recalculating the 1999 votes, the answer is that the Liberal Democrats would have kept their ten seats, Labour would have lost three and the Tories two, with the minor parties sharing the remaining losses. This was before the UKIP surge.

In practice, the Conservatives lost nine, reducing from 36 down to 27, an additional net loss of seven. The reason was that this time UKIP gained nine seats, jumping from three to 12. The majority of their gains were at the direct expense of the Conservatives. This reduction in Conservative numbers had an immediate effect.

Committee Chairmanships in the European Parliament, positions of real authority, are allocated by nationality on the basis of the relative strength in number of MEPs. In 1999 Conservatives comprised one of the largest national delegations from any Member State – second only to the German Christian Democrats. On that basis we were then allocated two Chairmanships: Environment (the largest and most important) and Fisheries (particularly important to the UK).

In 2004, with reduced numbers, Conservatives only got one Chairmanship – namely Industry. Certainly this is an important Committee, which now has a strong Conservative Chairman in Giles Chichester MEP. But there was to be no second Chairmanship: the earlier Chairmanship of the Fisheries Committee had to be surrendered to the French, with the senior Vice-Chairman being Spanish. Such a result has hardly been a triumph for the UK national interest.

When it comes to votes, most of the proposed Directives affect the UK directly and the devil can be in the detail. UKIP are not interested in the Directives, let alone the detail. That leaves the UK interest under-represented by their 12 votes.

Admittedly UKIP MEPs do usually vote in the plenary sessions in Strasbourg. MEPs have to record votes there in person in order to get their expenses paid. But generally that appears to be their only motivation for such a vote: it is usually either an abstention or a No vote on principle regardless of the issue.

UKIP maintains that the European Parliament simply does not matter – or if it does, it ought not to. Representatives of UK companies and trade organisations know otherwise. They are frequently over in Brussels to talk to MEPs, guiding them on the regulatory frameworks they wish to see determined at EU level in order to produce a level business playing-field. MEPs have the powers to shape such laws. Detailed work is needed to try and get them right.

UKIP MEPs play little part in committees where the real work is done. The new face of UKIP, MEP Robert Kilroy-Silk, said publicly that he wasn't going to waste time going to Brussels to get bogged down in committees.

Whatever the reason for their non-involvement, the result is that the UK national interest is seriously weakened. The views of the more federalist parties - with a very different political agenda - remain represented in strength.

The danger is that this can be repeated at a General Election. In some constituencies it has already happened.

In the 2001 Christopher Gill stood down as the maverick Conservative MP for Ludlow. He also left the Conservative Party to head up the Freedom Association. His attacks against his former party colleagues ensured a healthy Conservative majority was overturned. He was replaced by a Liberal Democrat, a member of a party that welcomes the Euro, welcomes the EU Constitution and welcomes handing over more powers from Westminster.

This result was a disaster scenario for everything UKIP professes to believe. Instead, UKIP smugly say it is somehow all the fault of the Tories and not UKIP's responsibility at all.

There have been similar results at local level. In October 2004 there was a key by-election for Malvern Hills District Council, for a seat formerly held by an Independent. It was a seat Conservatives needed to win. It was a seat Conservatives should have won. But then a former Conservative party member decided to stand for UKIP against the official Conservative candidate. The consequence was that the Conservative vote was split, and the official Tory came second to the Liberal Democrats – losing by a mere nine votes.

UKIP polled 46 votes and was instrumental in robbing the Conservatives of victory.

As a direct result of this extra seat, the LibDems won overall control of the Council.

Already the federalists throughout the country have got the message. If people can be encouraged to vote UKIP, especially in Conservative-held seats, it will be good news for Labour and the Liberal Democrats.

Essentially it will be good news for all those who believe we should move towards a more federal Europe.

This is the real achievement of UKIP voters. The stronger they become, the more they strengthen their worst enemies.

When Robert Kilroy-Silk finally flounced out of UKIP in January 2005 he announced: "There's no way I could ask people in all conscience to vote for UKIP because it would be defrauding them".

It is difficult to disagree.

CHAPTER 2

Europe sees Red

Instead of making protest votes in the UK, real votes are needed in Brussels.

For one very good reason. There is no single EU political agenda. There are distinctly different agendas from different Member States just as there are within the Commission and within the European Parliament. Each is competing for supremacy. A majority vote will determine the winner. Every vote matters.

The Conservative vision of light regulation and free markets is gaining in support, especially since the arrival of the ten new Member States who relish their new-found freedom. But the Old Left is still alive and well, and its main base is the major red-tape factory in the Commission called the Directorate of Employment and Social Affairs. Although this lays down rules limiting how long we can all work, it has itself been working overtime for years.

It owes its current clout to a key compromise necessary to

get the European Economic Community off the ground many years ago.

When the Common Market was first suggested, the Left saw it as a crusade for capitalism. If it prospered as expected, socialism would be squashed. That did not seem such a great idea to the Socialists across Europe.

The Left in Britain certainly didn't like it. When Edward Heath held the original vote in the House of Commons in favour of Common Market entry he proposed that MPs from all parties should have a free vote. Leading by example, he confirmed there would indeed be no party whip for the Conservatives. In contrast Harold Wilson insisted the Left should be whipped to vote against entry, and most Labour MPs needed no urging. They didn't like the idea of the Common Market one little bit.

Tony Blair didn't like it either. Years later when he was campaigning to become an MP for the first time, he put a promise to leave the EU at the top of his personal election manifesto. How times have changed.

The seeds of change were sown in the mid-80's, primarily by the Socialist Commission President Jacques Delors. The Single Market, as it was becoming known, was making only sluggish progress. The UK Conservative Commissioner Arthur Cockfield had recently laid down a very robust list of specific actions designed to spur it into life. Delors knew he needed to get the trade unions on-side in order to deliver it.

So in 1985, in order to buy their support, he proposed a formal process of regular Social Dialogue between the European Trade Union Confederation (ETUC), the Union of Industries of the European Community (UNICE) and the European Centre of Public Enterprises (CEEP). These would be known as the Social Partners. It was also agreed that the Social Partners would be asked by the Commission to consider controversial issues together, to see if the two sides of industry could come up with voluntary agreements to make legislation unnecessary. This also sounded a great idea.

The problem was that the Trade Unions soon cottoned on to the fact that if they registered a failure to agree, the Commission would have to go to the Council and say: the two sides of industry have failed to agree voluntarily on a certain issue, therefore most reluctantly the Commission had to propose legislation. Thus there was every pressure on employers to give in early in order to avoid new laws, and no pressure whatever on the union side to do any such thing.

It was also agreed to develop a 'European Social Model'. This entailed a high level of social protection for people out of work, and a high level of employee rights for those employed. Both would lead to rigid and inflexible labour markets and considerable on-costs for business. Both would also lead to official powers being assigned to the Trade Unions.

This social dimension was given formal authority in the

Single European Act of 1986. It would really take off a few years later in the Maastricht Treaty which called for consultation of the Social Partners to be legally compulsory in all areas of social affairs. The Unions had finally arrived.

Delors himself addressed a TUC Conference in Bournemouth in 1988. His speech amazed and delighted the delegates. He said the EU was much more than just a Common Market, abolishing barriers to trade. It should be designed "to benefit each and every citizen of the Community. It is therefore necessary to improve workers' living and working conditions, and to provide better protection for their health and safety at work."

The challenge was to give the Common Market a fully-fledged social dimension. The challenge was accepted with acclaim. Transport Workers' Union General Secretary Ron Todd admitted the Unions were being rolled back and rolled over in Westminster. In Brussels they would be on a roll themselves.

From now on the Left would be firmly in favour of the EU. It was indeed a decisive moment.

There was actually logic for some form of social dimension. The original argument ran that if you wanted a real Common Market, with all countries having equal opportunity to compete inside each other's domestic national market, then the country in the EU with the lowest overall costs would clean up. That could mean pressure for other Member States to squeeze wages, depress working conditions, and cut corners on health and safety so that they could lower their own costs and compete better. It could mean more company restructuring and redundancies or even back to the worst Victorian times, with children chased up chimneys while the rich got richer and the poor got poorer.

On the basis of this argument it was agreed there needed to be laws on social protection, universally applicable across the EU, to prevent what came to be known as 'social dumping' – the possible pressure for countries to downgrade to the lowest common social denominator. There needed to be some common Health & Safety rules so that there would be a level-playing field in terms of worker protection.

The problem was, and is, that the solution has become worse than the problem. In the real world, business success was never leading to downgrading of social and working conditions. Indeed by creating greater wealth it would produce the opposite. But the promotion of this social dimension has led to a raft of excessive and intrusive legislation, from which the only gainers have been the Trade Union movement.

Certainly John Monks, current President of the European Trade Union Confederation (ETUC), is now a very happy man. Today he is able to state with pride that "Under the European Treaty, the ETUC's status amounts to co-legislator on employment and social policy in the EU." In theory, the only co-legislators are the elected Parliament and the elected Member State Governments. In practice, the Unions are right up there alongside.

The real frustration, and one reason why so many people feel so overwhelmed with relentless and intrusive EU legislation, is that laws to unlock the Single Market can take years of negotiation to see the light of day whereas the social laws agreed to in part exchange have been pouring out without any delay at all.

Much of the Single Market jam will come long after tomorrow, yet much of the social regulatory pain is here right now.

This was and is a pretty lousy deal, and has to be addressed. Under the guise of promoting social justice, the European Social Model is instead blocking change, creating uncompetitive companies and pressure on employers to avoid taking new people on. The cost of employing people with all the social on-costs can be so high, and the costs of having to lay them off is even higher. This results in massive Continental unemployment – which is the biggest social injustice of all.

The trouble is that it has generated a momentum all of its own, and it is our very own UK Labour MEPs who are leading it.

In order to push this social agenda along, the European Trade Unions have encouraged their members to become MEPs. Most Socialist MEPs (and all UK Labour MEPs) are members of at least one trade union. All focus on the social agenda in the professed belief that this delivers happier and more productive workers and therefore greater competitiveness. They ignore the consequent result of the extra burdens on business, that continental European unemployment is approaching 10% and rising.

The Conservative approach is to liberate enterprise to create the wealth to pay for a strong social agenda. It is exactly the opposite way round.

The different visions of Europe were well described by Margaret Thatcher in her speech to the 1988 Conservative Party Conference:

"I welcome the debate, because it has brought into the open an equally fundamental question – the choice between two kinds of Europe: a Europe based on the widest possible freedom for enterprise; or a Europe governed by socialist methods of centralised control and regulation. There is no doubt what the Community's founders intended."

"The Treaty of Rome is a charter for economic liberty, which they knew was the essential condition for personal and political liberty. Today that founding concept is under attack from those who see European unity as a vehicle for spreading socialism. We haven't worked all these years to free Britain from the paralysis of Socialism only to see it creep in through the back door of central control and bureaucracy from Brussels. That wasn't what we joined the European Community for."

"Ours is the true European ideal. It is that ideal which will fire our campaign in the European election. That is why we must win every possible seat in the European Parliament for the Conservative cause. We shall point out that Britain has taken the lead in tackling practical issues in Europe which are of real benefit to people – reform of the Common Agricultural Policy, completion of the Single Market, the fight against terrorism and drugs; that Britain continues to make the second largest financial contribution to Europe; that Britain stations more forces beyond its borders – nearly seventy thousand of them – than any other European country in defence of freedom. With those sort of credentials no-one should doubt Britain's wholehearted commitment to Europe."

John Major saw the Socialist vision blossoming and tried to stop it. At Maastricht he obtained unanimous agreement from all the other EU Member States that the UK could opt out from the Social Chapter – which contained these stifling employment and social laws – thereby ring-fencing the country from the worst excesses of the Left. Sadly he was outmanoeuvred in one key area.

The European Court of Justice ruled that the Working Time Directive, whereby Brussels laid down how many hours people should graciously be permitted to work, was a Health & Safety measure rather than a simple piece of social legislation. If they worked too long they might get tired and this could be dangerous. The workers might not realise this themselves, which is why the EU had to step in and decide for them. And because Health & Safety had already been agreed by Member States as coming under Qualified Majority Voting, the UK was stuck with it despite our Social Chapter opt-out.

In the views of many, the idea that 'Brussels' should determine how many hours we can work, rest and play is an outrageous intrusion into our personal freedoms. Indeed it is one of the most often quoted reasons why we should walk away.

But even here the UK initially gained a key measure of flexibility, by retaining the right for individuals to exercise the right to opt-out themselves. If people wanted to work longer hours, and get paid the extra overtime that went with it, they were allowed the choice. However this too is now under threat.

Earlier in 2004 UK Labour MEPs each voted in favour of removing the individual opt-out "as soon as possible". The CBI said this would be disastrous. The UK Labour Government agreed and pleaded with Labour MEPs to leave the opt-out alone, but to no avail. Even the Commission did not propose to go as far as banning it completely, though it produced a plan to restrict the permitted use of the opt-out that would give the effective right of veto to a trade union even if the employee was not a union member. It was significant that this proposal was rushed in during the dying weeks of the outgoing left-led European Commission. Some of us will be pressuring the new Commission to leave well alone.

Meanwhile, the original Social Chapter opt-out had succeeded in two key respects. Not only did it shelter the UK from much of the rigidity stifling enterprise on the continent; it also slowed the continental appetite for more such legislation. So this was doubly good news.

That is, until Tony Blair came along.

Perhaps anxious to show penitence for his original anti-EU manifesto, one of his first acts on becoming Prime Minister was to sign up to the Social Chapter hook, line and sinker. Not only did this unleash pages of existing EU social legislation into the UK: it removed the worry other countries had about their becoming more uncompetitive vis-a-vis the UK. We would all be in the same boat together. So the dam which had held back further social legislation was demolished to let loose a new torrent of red tape. It is no wonder that ordinary people at the receiving end are now increasingly anti-EU.

The problem has been that Thatcher's portrayal of "the paralysis of Socialism" has not just been creeping in at the back door. The front door has been blasted wide open.

For 20 years since the first direct elections to the European Parliament back in the 70's the largest single party of MEPs was the Party of European Socialists (PES), mainly because the Right was split into different groups. For most of those years too, EU Member States had Leftish governments: these in turn appointed Left-wing Commissioners. So for year after year, the three key EU Institutions – the Parliament, the Council and the Commission – were Left/Left/Left. Socialist One-Size-Fits-All legislation was not just unchallenged but basically nodded through.

There is now a lot of it about.

The tide turned in 1999, when for the first time the largest political grouping in the Parliament was the Centre-Right. Since then, the majority of EU Member States (including some of the ten new Members) have converted to Centre-Right Governments: these have in turn appointed what we might describe as Conservative Commissioners – 17 out of the 25 are from the Right. These are determined to move the EU in a new direction. With a Right/Right/Right combination they finally have a real chance to succeed. Conservatives want to be in there to help.

But the Left have not given up. Because Health & Safety is one area where EU red tape is allowed to flourish, the MEP who acts as Socialist Co-ordinator for Employment & Social Affairs has called for new EU legislation on Workplace Bullying, a new Directive on Workplace Economics, for strengthening of the Display Screen Equipment Directive and for tightening the Manual Handling Directive. For good measure he urged a comprehensive extension of the Carcinogenic Agents Directive, and demanded a new Directive laying down minimum standards for the Recognition of Occupational Diseases.

This was all in a single speech.

Have we not got enough Health & Safety legislation at EU level? Apparently not, according to Labour politicians.

This Co-ordinator, who leads the whole 200-strong Socialist

Group on Employment issues, is a UK Labour MEP. He can truly say that Britain is influencing the agenda: the problem is that he is pushing for more red tape not less. The UK Government merely turns a blind eye and merrily lets him get on with it – while spinning in the national press that it is opposing it fiercely.

UKIP lump the major parties together as indistinguishable in wanting More Europe not Less. This is blatant nonsense. There has always been vivid blue water between Right and Left in Europe. Had the Right got its act together much earlier, and had the Right not been divided, the Left would not have done so well.

Those who have promoted such divisions within the Right have only themselves to blame.

It would be easy to say that the Right vision of Europe has lost the battle, that the Left is on the march, that the UK should give in and get out. That way we would certainly have lost. The Old Socialist model would be preserved in continental Europe, in our major market and on our very doorstep. It would not just be their problem: it would be our problem too.

The solution is to join forces against the enemy, not to find fault with our friends. Our friends are in the European People's Party.

CHAPTER 3

Reigning in Spain

The European People's Party (EPP) has national party affiliates in most EU countries. The Spanish component is known as the Partido Popular, or PP for short. This party is strong throughout Spain and the Balearic islands, though in some areas it has historically settled for a distant second place behind the Socialists.

One such place was sunny Majorca, where British expatriates were particularly unhappy. They had three main gripes.

The first was that together with the Germans they made up nearly 25% of the local population, yet there was nobody on the local Councils to represent their interests.

The second was that they were encouraged to become residents, to live and pay taxes. But their special Resident's card which entitled them to stay was stamped 'foreigner'. This meant they were not allowed a vote in any local or national elections.

The third was that they were often stuck living in areas

under Socialist-controlled councils where the public services got poorer as the taxes got higher. They had Taxation without Representation, and that had been the basis for the American Revolution.

The Association of Foreign Citizens favoured a more peaceful response, but were no less determined. They lobbied hard the left-wing Government of Felipe Gonzales in Madrid to be allowed to have a vote in time for the 1995 local Council elections. They felt they were close to success when Gonzales made a landmark speech. He said: "The time has come and gone for political platitudes and lip service to the principles of the European Union. An estimated 25 million Europeans living outside their country of birth are being denied their rights at the ballot box. Their voice must be heard sooner or later."

It was to be later.

Nothing happened.

Fortunately the Government changed and so did the answer. Success finally arrived in 1999 under Prime Minister Jose Maria Aznar of the Partido Popular who gave the all-clear at least for Council elections.

Some 6,500 expats throughout Majorca voted in the election that followed, but on this occasion were not enough to make any difference to the result. They remained unrepresented, and frankly felt there was little they could do so there was no point in trying.

Enter Peter Newey and Kate Mentink.

Both were expat UK Conservatives living in the Calvia Borough Council area, not far from the capital Palma. Peter was the dynamic former Chairman of Sutton Coldfield Conservative Association back in the UK. He was an entrepreneur, running a successful local restaurant, and was determined to use his energies to make a difference. He had long had his eye on Kate Mentink, a fluent Dutch and German-speaking live-wire Scot who had been Founder Chairman of Ciudados Europeos (European Citizens), an organisation representing the many different expatriate nationalities that had since spread throughout the island.

He had suggested to her many times that she should stand as a Councillor in the 2003 elections on behalf of the Partido Popular, the official Centre-Right opposition to the ruling Socialist clique. The idea that an expat candidate might win a seat where successive Spanish Conservative candidates had consistently failed over the previous twenty years seemed far-fetched. But when one day she was officially approached by Carlos Delgado, the PP nominee for mayor should the party ever win control, she finally agreed.

That was the easy decision. The real challenge was to get her elected.

With all his UK campaigning experience, Peter saw the need to build up a dedicated team from scratch. Kate provided a room and within a short time a bank of telephones was manned, two shifts a day, six days a week, fully twelve months ahead of Election Day. The objective was to speak to all the expatriates in person, and mobilise each one to get onto the electoral register and actively support the campaign.

The main task was establishing the belief that the massive Socialist majority really could be overthrown, and that they could do the overthrowing.

They held meetings and social events. They mounted rallies. Spanish PP Councillors came out in support. Kate personally attended every event and spread herself everywhere, and not just within the British community. It was a tribute to the way she touched others that, in the final weeks of the campaign, telephones were also manned by German expatriates who often spoke no English at all. There were 102 different nationalities on the island: the task was to reach out to them all. They signed up nearly 2,200 expats in the Calvia region alone.

They then spent further hours following up registration forms that mysteriously went missing in the local Town Hall. This was no great surprise. Meanwhile various local businesses supporting the PP were threatened with unscheduled visits from various inspectors who would contrive reasons to close them down unless they backed off. This was no surprise either. At the time of the election there were to be no less than seven criminal charges of fraud against the Socialist Mayoress personally. Local taxes had risen to be the highest in the Balearic islands, if not in Spain itself, but nobody seemed sure where all the money was spent. But everyone was aware that from being one of the richest municipalities in the whole of Spain, two decades of left-wing rule had left Calvia technically bankrupt. But the expectation was that the Socialists would still win again. They always did.

Not this time. The campaign team's efforts were to be handsomely rewarded. Kate achieved a record overall vote of 6,700 for the PP on the day, just taking the seat with a majority of 200 votes. The Mayoress lost her seat and her job. It was to be all change in Calvia.

The PP had achieved the impossible. Spanish PP supporters had rallied round, but the expats had made the difference.

The old line-up had given the Socialists control with 11 out of the 21 available seats, with the PP getting nine and with one Independent. This time around the Socialists dropped to nine and lost their majority. The PP gained the Calvia seat to become the largest party, and now run the Council. Kate is the first expat Councillor in the whole of Spain. She got there with the help of her friends.

Some might still say: why did she need the Partido Popular? She could surely have fought as an Independent and later serve alongside the new Centre-Right ruling coalition?

No she couldn't. The Centre-Right would not be ruling.

Had Kate stood as an Independent in this particular seat

there would also have been a separate PP candidate. The Conservative vote would have been split. The Socialists would have kept the seat and kept control.

But Kate did more than just get elected. By working within the Partido Popular she was immediately appointed to a key new post. She is now officially the Councillor for Tourism and Foreign Relations. She is in a position to make a difference, and she sure is making it.

There is already a department dedicated to non-Spanish people. There is a new local radio station broadcasting in English and German. A commitment to reduce local taxes by 5% each year has been widely acclaimed. The Spanish as well as non-Spanish are noticing how matters have improved. There could be a real chance of further gains in 2007.

The moral is that working closely with the local EPP party achieved real success against the Socialists in a single local Council.

Is it not possible – just possible – that working with the EPP in Brussels might help roll back the Left on the wider European stage?

CHAPTER 4

To EPP or not to EPP

The lie that all major UK political parties are equally 'federalist' in failing to stand up for Britain in Europe is regularly peddled by UKIP supporters. But they were reinforced in their cause by a newspaper that historically had been a friend to the Tories, but had now effectively decided to endorse the UKIP line.

Just days before the European Parliamentary elections of June 2004, The *Daily Telegraph* published a major feature article by Charles Moore. It unsettled many Conservative members and was widely welcomed by UKIP. The opening remarks are worth quoting at length:

"Like, I suspect, a good many people reading this article, I am hoping to vote Conservative in the European elections next week. My reasons are fairly simple: I don't like the Labour Government, I agree with the Tory opposition to the European Constitution and the euro, I think Michael Howard is an able leader and, besides, I am by nature a Tory. But Mr Howard's party is not making it very easy for me. At the European Parliament, the British Conservatives are in alliance with the European People's Party. I have just read the EPP programme, drawn up this year. The EPP believes in 'developing the EU into a political Union'. It wants a 'federal Europe' (albeit a 'decentralised' one). It supports co-ordinated taxation across the EU, and opposes national immigration policies. It calls for the institution of a European public prosecutor, and for political oversight of European policing by the European Parliament. It says that schools should teach a 'European civic spirit'.

"All member states must join the euro, it says, and a Common Foreign and Security Policy must be fully integrated into EU structures, with the European Rapid Reaction Force as its 'armed component'. The EPP supports the ratification of the European Constitution for 'the good functioning of the enlarged Europe'. I don't want any of these things. In fact, they are an almost comprehensive list of the things I don't want. No blame attaches to the EPP for these policies: they are the natural views of a party which has always supported ever deeper European integration. It just seems strange that the Tory party should be teaming up with this lot. Ask more questions and it gets stranger still. It turns out that the Tories had the opportunity to lead a new political grouping at the European Parliament which would have included parties from the new member states such as Poland, and would have been atlanticist and Euro-sceptic. This party would have been the third largest in the parliament. But these negotiations were dropped, and instead the Tories made a new agreement with the EPP. The idea is that the Tories can sit and vote separately, but they get all the taxpayers' money which the European parliament doles out for staff, research etc, through the EPP. The EPP skims a percentage off to campaign for europhile causes – things like a 'yes' vote in the Swedish euro referendum – and gives the rest to the Tories. Some Tories think this is all very clever. Others think it is a necessary price to pay for 'the deal', a pact, they whisper, between Mr Howard and his old Cambridge friend Kenneth Clarke to maintain peace between Right and Left in the Tory Party. But for the voter, it produces a political party which makes Euro-sceptic noises, but takes europhile money, says it opposes the Constitution and the Euro, but links up with one of their biggest promoters. When the UK Independence Party comes along and says that the main parties are 'deceitful', it is hard to disagree."

This is powerful stuff.

Given that the overall Conservative party, including its MEPs, also regard the 'comprehensive list' referred to above as things we don't want either, what on earth are we up to? There ought to be a good explanation.

There is.

It is the product of a policy initiated under Margaret Thatcher's premiership, developed under John Major's, and extended under the leadership of William Hague. It is nothing to do with money. It is nothing to do with any supposed pact between Michael Howard and Kenneth Clarke as there is no such pact. It has nothing to do with diluting or compromising the Conservative vision of Europe as promoting freedom, prosperity and opportunity. It is everything to do with turning that vision into reality.

Conservative MEPs are not members of the European People's Party (EPP). We are allied members of a political Group that includes the EPP, but is in fact made up of some 59 separate national parties from the various EU member states. The fact that there are 59 parties from only 25 countries may look like a typing error: in fact it illustrates the nature of the political Group.

It consists of a number of separate parties from France and Italy, for example, that stand against each other in their national elections for the European Parliament (fighting on their own separate manifestoes), but that nonetheless choose to sit with each other in the same umbrella grouping once they are elected – before standing against each other again in their home countries five years down the line.

Despite their differences, they come together in the Parliament in one overriding common cause. They want to fight the real enemy, the Party of European Socialists (PES), whose vision of a prescriptive One-Size-Fits-All Europe is anathema to them all.

Until 1999, the PES was the largest single political grouping in the European Parliament. Although it never had an absolute majority, it dominated the agenda because its opponents on the Centre-Right were divided and weakened. As the main Centre-Right progressively got its act together, it became a 'broader church' by reaching out to other centre-right parties including the UK Conservatives. The EPP Group is now the largest political grouping by a significant margin (268 members, 68 ahead of the PES).

It has no overall majority either, but a sign of its current clout came in mid-2004 when candidates lined up to be the new President of the European Commission. The Leader of the EPP Group laid it on the line that the new President had to reflect the political geography following the June elections, in other words had to be from the Centre-Right. After much initial resistance from the Socialist-led countries, this was accepted. President José Manuel Barroso from Portugal looks like being exactly the strong, principled and reformist that Conservatives have long sought for this role.

An earlier example of using the collective clout is closer to home. After the tragedy of the Foot and Mouth epidemic in the UK, Tony Blair refused to hold a public enquiry into the handling of the outbreak for the obvious reason that he had no wish to see the Government's mismanagement of it publicly paraded for all to see. Because of the movement of livestock across borders, the outbreak had potential impact on Denmark, France and Germany in particular. There was considerable EU concern that such an outbreak should never be allowed to happen again or, if it did, that it should be dealt with in a far more effective manner.

It was the Conservative Agriculture Spokesman in the European Parliament who conceived the idea of setting up a formal EU Committee of Public Enquiry, which would have the power to summon ministers to account for their actions. However, to secure such a Committee required 150 MEPs to sign a written declaration demanding it. With only 36 UK Conservative MEPs at the time, we could never have achieved this on our own. With the backing of our EPP colleagues within the group we had over 200 signatures inside two days. Within two weeks every other political grouping had joined the bandwagon – except of course the Party of European Socialists. The Enquiry took place, and with great effect.

Charles Moore cherry-picked some aspects he (and we) did not like about the individual EPP manifesto. He could have chosen instead to list the specific EPP Group priorities for the 2004-2009 legislative term of the European Parliament, as declared by the EPP Congress in February 2004, which present a very different message. I happily quote them in full with no editing:

"Attentive to the expectations of European citizens, the EPP identifies the following themes as their most important concerns:
1   securing jobs and incomes;
2   all aspects of threats to safety and health;
3   the possibility of all groups of society to take part in society, especially in the labour market;
4   environmental deterioration;
5   the consequences of bad government and socialist

economic policies (inequality, poverty, epidemics, civil war);

6   good governance by the public authorities, notably through the reduction of the tax burden crippling entrepreneurial efforts."

These are the EPP Group parliamentary priorities for MEPs. They are priorities for the UK Conservative MEPs too. They require major changes in the way the EU does business, changes to be fought for every step of the way. Conservatives will be fighting in the front line.

The authors of such priorities are not our enemies: they are on our side against the real enemy.

Later on in this same document, there are elaborations of these priorities. These include the following remarks:

'Unemployment' is unjust. We believe that the human being, his/her motivation, qualification, creativity and ability to innovate, are at the core of our economic and social policy. That means a consistent reduction in unemployment is the best social policy and an important expression of solidarity. Unlike the Socialists, who prefer bureaucratic regulations and state interventions, we create the right conditions for more – and more secure – jobs, ensuring favourable conditions for free enterprise throughout Europe. For us, competition is one of the most important sources of entrepreneurial initiative, innovation, investments and prosperity.....

More important is economic growth, which we will only achieve if we transform Europe into a more dynamic and more competitive economic region. That is the reason why we are committed to reducing trade barriers and liberalising markets......"

How could Conservatives have a problem allying ourselves to such a philosophy? It would be a much bigger problem, and a present to our Socialist opponents, if we were to deny our support.

Margaret Thatcher said in her address to the Senate of the Polish Republic in 1991: "I have seen in other European countries what happens when reformers of the centre-right do not work together. Fragmentation has been a prescription for powerlessness."

Powerlessness of the Right simply gifts more power to the Left. That has been the sorry saga in Europe until 1999 and the Right has only itself to blame. Conservatives yearn to wield power in Europe, to drive change in Europe, to attack and roll back Socialism in Europe. Working together in this common cause is the only sure way to secure it.

It is worth adding that many of the key issues raised by Charles Moore – a Common Foreign & Security Policy, a European Public Prosecutor, a European Army, tax coordination, political union – are matters primarily for the national Governments of Member States to decide in the European Council, not MEPs in the European Parliament. That is why there was no mention of any of them whatever in the list of Group Parliamentary priorities listed in full above. Such issues are above and beyond the powers granted to mere MEPs.

However, because this is clearly not well understood – not least by Charles Moore – Conservatives have been careful to be precise about the terms of the alliance within the European Parliament. The full name of the political group is the Group of the European People's Party (Christian Democrats) and European Democrats, or EPP/ED for short. The current tally of 27 UK Conservatives (since the 2004 election) comprise the bulk of the ED element. The balance includes one Ulster Unionist, one Italian from the Pensioners' Party, two Portuguese from the Partido Popular and nine members of the Czech Civic Democrats making an additional 13 MEPs and an overall ED membership of 40.

Charles Moore said that the Conservatives had the opportunity to "lead a new political grouping at the European Parliament which would have included parties from the new member states such as Poland, and would have been atlanticist and Euro-sceptic".

We did and we do.

But he added that this could have been the third largest political group in the Parliament.

It couldn't and it isn't.

Conservatives maintain a clear 'ED' identity within the group with no compromise to our principles. In fact our independence is specifically secured under an article in the rules drafted by us which states: "The Members under this Article have the right to promote and develop their distinct views on constitutional and institutional issues in relation to the future of Europe."

One side-benefit of the clarity of these new rules is that some former EPP members, namely the UDF from France with eleven members and the Italian Christian Democrats with four, have promptly left the Group in high dudgeon to join the ultra-federalist European Liberal Democrat group. They complain that the EPP is not sufficiently federalist any more as a result of the UK Conservative pressure – no mean achievement of our membership in itself.

Our colleagues from the Centre-Right across the EU are very clear where we stand. As the largest political party representing the UK for the second successive election, Conservatives have put themselves in the strongest position to deliver.

But we do not just shelter within the Group and then go our own separate way. We also seek to influence the whole Group more to our way of thinking.

We have secured several positions as 'EPP/ED Co-ordinator' on key committees, with the authority to allocate parliamentary reports and set the overall voting whip for the Group. We hold more such important positions in this Group than any other nationality apart from the Germans.

Conservatives are also setting the pace in other ways. A South East region MEP James Elles conceived the idea of a Centre-Right think-tank under the auspices of the Group to develop new policies more appropriate to the needs of the day. Called the European Ideas Network, it was launched as a Summer University at Oxford in 2002. It moved to Madrid for 2003, and then on to Berlin in 2004 by which time it had grown to over 300 participants. Recent political speakers have included Carl Bildt from Sweden, Jose-Maria Aznar from Spain and Angela Merkel from Germany. Business-people, journalists and professors have come from all over the world to contribute.

The Secretary-General of the Konrad Adenauer Stiftung has described James as "not just the spiritual father of the European Ideas Network but its driving force". Conservatives are not just pulling our own weight: we are having success in pulling the whole Centre-Right alongside us.

As Charles Moore concludes in his final paragraph:

> "What we need, therefore, is a big, old, grown-up political party, preferably with a system of allies in other member states, developing the doctrine and detail of renegotiation, of opting out, of fighting back. The Tory party is the only vehicle qualified by history to do this."

With this paragraph at least Conservatives can agree. It is of course precisely what we are doing.

Ironically it is probably the very reason why UKIP focuses its attack on the Conservatives rather than the two federalist parties. If the Conservatives succeed in reforming the EU from within, then by definition UKIP has no case and no future. UKIP need us to fail.

CHAPTER 5

The Uncommon Market

The test of success will come with the completion of the Common Market, where Conservatives have led the charge since the beginning.

One frustration is that it is taking such a long time to complete. Another is that its delivery requires so many new rules.

This may sound a contradiction in terms. Surely Free Trade should mean that rules should be removed? Exactly so!

It does mean the removal of individual national rules, but it also means their replacement by a single set of EU rules. This is much easier said than done.

The Common Market is certainly about freedom, or four freedoms to be precise. The founding principle is that Goods, People, Money and Services should each have full freedom of movement across national borders. But such freedoms are not technicalities, to be readily resolved by the stroke of a pen. They are fundamentally political issues, in that they strike at the heart of Member States' national policies on public ownership, state aid, protectionism, competition and the management of the economy. That is why so much political effort is needed to make the Market happen.

Goods can now cross borders, widening consumer choice and reducing prices. Before individual national frontiers came down, there were 60 million customs clearance documents every year within the EU, plus queues at the borders. Now there are none. But many individual categories still bump up against other barriers.

People can now cross borders: more than 15 million EU citizens now work, or have retired, to another EU country. 1 million students have attended another EU college or university. But equal qualifications are not always recognised as equal: many jobs still remain closed to non-nationals.

Money can certainly cross borders, as the giant takeover of the German Mannesmann by Vodafone clearly showed. But again different pension rules, insurance regulations etc., prevent some funds from flowing freely. The important market for Financial Services is only just being opened up.

Finally the market for Services overall, including Telecommunications as well as Energy and accounting for 60% of the EU economy, is still in its infancy. Eliminating the remaining barriers here could boost cross-border trade in services by up to 20%.

The original concept of a Common Market seemed so very simple. Just phase out all the different tariffs and customs duties that are barriers to free trade and hey presto! you are there.

The EU has done all that, but we are still not there. That was the easy bit. For any market to be free there has to be a single set of detailed rules to ensure the playing-field is level. That can be a problem in itself: how many rules do you need, who decides them and who is the referee? But the reason we are still short of a genuinely Common Market is not because there are too many EU rules. It is because different countries are deciding the rules differently – or are ignoring them – and that the referee is not yet fully effective.

The Common Market is still not yet common. It does not yet deliver equal benefits to all consumers and businesses in every Member State. There are more than 1,500 infringement cases before the European Court of Justice, cases where certain countries are ignoring or by-passing agreed EU rules.

Many Member States have also kept restrictive trade barriers in place. These are the so-called non-tariff barriers, deliberately erected and maintained by different countries to protect their own domestic markets. Only when these are demolished will the Common Market be finally completed. If the EU did not exist, they would simply stay up. Only pressure from other Member States within the EU will tear them down, replacing them with a single secure legal EU framework so that companies, large and small, can reap economies of scale. We should be making it as easy for them to do business in another Member State as it is in their own. We are not yet there.

One after the other these individual non-tariff barriers are indeed being dismantled, but sometimes painfully slowly. A perfect example of such a barrier, and such a painfully slow process, is Chocolate.

Ever since the UK joined the Common Market back in 1973, British Dairy Milk Chocolate could not be legally sold throughout the EU. It was not locked out by price, or by high customs duties – a Free Trade Area could readily take care of these. It was locked out because the product did not conform to the official quality standards defined by the original six Member States. Later to be joined by Spain and Greece, these countries outlawed chocolate containing vegetable fat being sold in Europe as 'Chocolate'.

The remaining seven countries, including the UK, could carry on producing chocolate with up to 5% vegetable fat for home consumption. But home did not include the other eight countries of the so-called Single Market. The original 'Cadbury' formula of 20% cocoa solids and 20% milk solids was cheaper to make, and might therefore undermine the sales of the much more expensive 'continental' chocolate. So it had to be locked out.

In 1996 Commission pressure for change produced a so-called compromise permitting milk chocolate to be sold everywhere, as long as the name changed to 'vegelate'. Understandably, this was swiftly binned by the British and Irish. Other unattractive proposals followed, with the same fate.

Finally the Germans were persuaded to change sides. They belatedly realised that the traditional continental recipe could only produce traditional chocolate. Innovation, which was driving market growth elsewhere in the world with 'aerated' products for example, positively required greater use of vegetable fats. Flexibility could be good business and they didn't want to miss out. The old coalition crumbled, though the French made a final attempt to keep the status quo by appealing to the European Parliament. They failed.

The solution was not to be harmonisation of recipe, with different kinds of chocolate being forced to contain an identical mix of ingredients. It was to be mutual recognition of the different national chocolate-making traditions. The consumer would be free to choose. That was after all what the Single Market was supposed to be all about.

The whole process had taken 28 years.

The moral is that you secure change – in the end – from the inside. It takes time, often a great deal of time, and there is still much to be done.

I have been personally surprised to discover that the one key EU institution really pushing for change has been the

European Commission itself, in trying to deliver the four freedoms as originally agreed by Member States.

The Commission has begun opening up the market for public procurement, so that national Governments can no longer protect their own national suppliers. It is significant that when the City of Strasbourg wanted a new mass transit tram system they finally chose a supplier in Derby. When the European Parliament wanted a single supplier for crockery it went to Stoke-on-Trent. None of this would have happened without the Commission.

One major Services sector is Telecommunications. Here Britain led the way with the original Conservative privatisation of British Telecom, which immediately brought prices down. This approach to opening up previously protected State monopolies is today the accepted wisdom throughout the EU. Prices have come down everywhere in consequence.

Mobile phone costs have also reduced. Europe has now developed a single operating standard for GSM mobile phones, compared to the three standards in the USA. One single regulatory standard has been established throughout all Member States, compared with some 80 different standards in America where so much is still done at individual State level. As a result, EU households have more mobiles than their US counterparts. Europe has led the way, giving major competitive advantage to EU suppliers.

Another important Services sector is Energy. Under EU law all 25 Member States should have completely opened up their national markets for business customers for electricity and natural gas by July 2004. 18 of the 25 missed the deadline. People in the UK often believe that the British are always the good guys at complying, with everyone else ignoring the rules. One of the 18 countries failing to comply on time was the United Kingdom.

There are other problems too. Italy, Portugal and Spain, geographically at the outer edges of the continent, have few physical energy links with other countries. In 2003, power prices in Italy were over 50% higher than the UK. Some might say this is Italy's problem. If there are blockages within the Single Market, it is a problem for all Market members.

The Commission is also pushing to open up the market for Financial Services, so that pensions are more portable across borders and insurance products can be offered more widely and more cheaply throughout the EU. Given the UK's strength in this huge sector it is very much in our interest that the market is opened up rapidly. This is a particular challenge given the current lack of common financial and regulatory rules across Member States.

The Commission has led the way in making it easier to effect cross-border mergers and takeovers, so that companies can seek the advantages of scale in an increasingly competitive global market. Not all companies are keen.

In October 2004 the Commission launched a legal challenge against the German car-maker Volkswagen. A national German law protects it from external takeover, which the Commission claims prevents the free movement of capital throughout the EU. This law specifies that no investor can have more than 20% of voting rights and that the regional government of Lower Saxony must have seats on the supervisory board. The previous Commission made loud noises about doing something, but stopped short of action. The incoming Commission is determined to act.

National protection might appear to be a Good Thing. This might have prevented our UK car manufacturers being bought by non-UK companies – including the ultimate Great British brand of Rolls-Royce. But the result of our freer market has been that the UK now makes and exports more cars than ever. Meanwhile, Volkswagen makes more cars in India than it does in Germany: national protection leads to uncompetitive national production.

Another major barrier to international competitiveness is the lack of a Single European Patent, so that people can protect their bright ideas in one document across Europe instead of the cost and complexity of doing it 25 times – and in different languages. Even French industrialists agree that there should be a single language, and that this should of course be English. It is French politicians who are putting nationalism above competitiveness by insisting on French as well – thereby triggering pleas for equal treatment led by the Germans and Spanish. The Commission continues to push.

Another cause of uncompetitiveness is State Aid – selective Government hand-outs to their own national champions that disadvantage companies from outside, or unfair bribes to one selected company to invest in a particular area. The bad news is that such State Aid topped 82 billion Euros in 2000. The good news is that eight years earlier it had been 104 billion. The Commission has been active here too.

It has ordered Spain to recover over 70 million Euros given to Daewoo in tax breaks and subsidies as an incentive to build a refrigeration manufacturing plant in the Basque region. It has compelled Germany to change a law preventing private mail-preparation companies from receiving the same discounts granted to bulk-mailers who feed self-prepared mail directly into Deutsche Post sorting centres. It has forced a change in the pricing policy of regional airports, whereby Charleroi in Belgium had given preferential landing charges of just one Euro per passenger to Ryanair, benefits offered to no other airline. There are increasing examples of such decisive action.

If anything we need the Commission to be even more active, especially to bring the French into line. If and when there is a 'Single European Sky', with national frontiers in the air opened up in parallel to the opening of borders on the ground, French air traffic controllers will no longer be able to hold air-travellers to ransom at peak holiday times. If penalties for flouting agreed EU laws were tightened, France will never again be able to ban British beef for years. If mutual recognition of professional qualifications became a reality across all Member States, French ski instructors will no longer enjoy a teaching monopoly in French resorts.

There is still much work to be done to drive change.

For the UK to leave the EU would simply slow the reform process. We need to be in there to speed it up.

The irony is that even when playing-fields are levelled, UKIP still contrive to complain. In December 2004 the Shrewsbury UKIP Chairman issued a torrent of abuse about an EU Directive, allegedly coming into force in 1st January 2005, which apparently ruled that the colour coding on wiring would change so that the black neutral wire became the live wire, and the red live wire became neutral. This was nonsense, but still made the news.

What had actually happened was that an organisation called CENELEC (The EU Committee for Electro-technical Standardisation), working with technical experts in 28 European countries, had issued a set of voluntary standards to which national Governments chose to sign up. These changes will take full effect in April 2006. For domestic wiring the changes will actually be: Brown for live, Blue for neutral, and Green/Yellow for earth.

This will bring wiring across the EU exactly into line with the colours used for flexes for UK domestic appliances since way back in 1968. There will also be changes for commercial cabling used in 3-phase installations.

The UKIP Chairman wondered how many poor unfortunates would be electrocuted by this 'EU madness'. There was no such madness, except from him. UK industry had been in the lead in pressing for all these changes. It is a huge step forward, for consumers as well as business.

Equally misrepresented has been the issue of the straightness of bananas, where there has indeed been an EU ruling. The Commission's job is to protect consumers from being fobbed off with substandard products anywhere in the EU. Hence their fruity suggestion under Regulation 2257/94 that as a minimum requirement bananas should be free from malformation or abnormal curvature of the fingers.

The UK had its own separate law on bendy bananas well before this EU regulation. So did other EU countries. But in each country it was expressed differently. The new regulation defined one single standard across the EU, addressing the underlying problem that abnormal curvature was a sign of a diseased plant. We may mock its message, but this regulation actually helped produce a Common Market for healthy and tasty bananas and removed a complexity of different national rules.

Please do not tell anyone about this.

It would be a shame to let the facts get in the way of a good story.

Nonetheless, this tale has a message for Ukippers. If they think there can be a single Common Market without detailed rules, then it is they who have gone bananas.

Alternatively, if they think countries can bypass all these rules by staying outside – just ask Norway.

CHAPTER 6

Should Norway be Our Way?

People often describe the European Union as the largest Single Market in the world. But few seem to know how large it really is.

The Single Market is usually considered as comprising the 25 EU Member States – 15 from 'Old Europe', plus the ten countries that joined in May 2004: Cyprus, Malta, Latvia, Lithuania, Estonia, Hungary, Poland, Slovenia, Slovakia and the Czech Republic.

It actually consists of 28, as it includes Norway, Iceland and Liechtenstein.

True, the last three countries are not members of the European Union. But they are nonetheless full members of the Single Market as a result of being signatories to a document called the European Economic Agreement.

They have access to a huge free trade area. They retain their national sovereignty. They would seem to have the best of all worlds. Maybe the UK should follow suit.

Or could there possibly be a downside?

Indeed there could.

The European Economic Agreement is a lengthy document with a stream of even longer annexes. However its essence is clear from the opening paragraph, appropriately titled Article 1. This states:

> "The aim of this Agreement of association is to promote a continuous and balanced strengthening of trade and economic relations between the contracting parties with equal conditions of competition, and respect of the same rules, with a view to creating a homogeneous European Economic Area, hereinafter referred to as the EEA".

The words "equal conditions" and "same rules" are key. They simply mean that the three countries signed up not only to all the EU legislation existing at the time: they committed to accepting all new legislation without question into the future.

There are two important exceptions, fishing and agriculture, of which fishing is the most important. Iceland's economy in particular is dependent on a successful fishing industry. Given that the EU's Common Fisheries Policy is generally agreed to be a disaster, both in terms of savaging an industry as well as failing to conserve fish stocks, Iceland's determination to go its own way thus far has been quite understandable.

In Iceland fish has always meant money. In fact dried fish doubled up as money for over 400 years, being legal tender well into the last century. As their Prime Minister has made clear recently: "The North Atlantic States depend upon fisheries for a living. They have managed, not without sacrifice, to build sustainable fisheries with an efficient industry. It is impossible for them to give up control over the fisheries resource to enter into a system that does not work."

Over 60% of all Iceland's current exports are marine products. The UK fisheries industry, important though it is, is significantly smaller. It is much smaller still, of course, as a result of the Common Fisheries Policy (CFP). That is why, as the former legal owners of over half the fishing grounds now allocated to the EU, the UK is leading the campaign to change the policy radically (that is to say the Conservatives are, but then so we should as it was us that ceded control in the first place).

Norway's economy is different, with fish and seafood accounting for only 5% of its exports. Agriculture is restricted, with only 3% of the land being arable: coupled with an unfriendly climate, Norwegian farmers are simply uncompetitive with the rest of the EU, and might not survive if the market was opened up. Although relatively few people now work on the land, this is a sensitive issue even for townsfolk.

Although the EEA signatories are outside the CFP and the Common Agricultural Policy (CAP), the EU has not relinquished all controls.

The EU is allowed to catch 3000 tonnes of redfish in Icelandic waters. It has laid down specific quotas for fish imports from the EEA to the ten new Member States, replacing the free trade arrangements that operated prior to their joining. In addition, all three countries have to conform to the food safety/food hygiene/veterinary standards and controls that are mandatory throughout the EU. But these countries have no powers whatever to affect how these standards and controls are determined.

More importantly, they have no powers to affect any other EU legislation either. They have a right to be consulted when the laws are being drawn up, but they have no votes during the process and no right of appeal afterwards. They have to comply fully with the laws as presented to them on a plate.

These laws cover the full range of Single Market issues. They include all the legislation on employment and health & safety. The dreaded Working Time Directives apply in full to them, and outside inspections are regularly conducted by an organisation with the forbidding title of the EFTA Surveillance Authority to make sure that EU laws are strictly observed.

In this context it is interesting to note the current status of one suggested EU law, at present blocked in the European Council. Titled the Atypical Workers' Directive, this would place strict new rules on temporary agency workers that according to the CBI could put over 160,000 temporary jobs at risk in the UK alone. Unusually the UK has been in a minority of Member States on this issue. But fortunately the UK has nonetheless been able to put together a coalition of three large countries and five smaller ones sufficient to block any such Directive happening — so far.

If just one large country were to defect, the blocking minority would be incomplete. Qualified Majority Voting would kick in and the Directive would go ahead.

If the UK were not a member of the EU, the blocking minority would be indeed be precisely one large country short.

Us.

And we would then indeed be stuck with the Directive: inside the EU we can do something about it.

If we were outside the EU we could do nothing to stop this legislation, yet we would still be bound by it. This would guarantee us the worst of both worlds. It is clear which position gives us more 'sovereignty'.

Meanwhile the idea that the UK is such a big trade player, that if we left the EU we could still demand exemption from such laws sounds so simple. It is not remotely realistic. If the EU allowed a back door open into its markets without its rules being applied, then why would anybody still play by the rules and use the front door? Do we really think the French or the Germans would play ball? Logically such an option cannot be possible. To do business with the EU on insider terms you have to be inside.

Some EU laws have a disproportionate impact on outsiders. Laws on safety inside road tunnels are particularly relevant to Norway, given its many mountains. Environmental legislation such as the Water Framework Directive is pertinent to Iceland: should it really be necessary for Iceland to go to the effort and the cost of surveying and assessing all its natural springs for water purity, when the whole island is blessed with an abundance of the purest supply?

The EU will listen, but is not obliged to hear. It is the EEA signatories who are meekly obliged to hear and to obey, and they do this rather well.

A recent analysis has ranked all countries on how best they comply with EU legislation. Top of the list is Norway, and it is not even in the EU.

There is also a physical price to pay for being outside. EEA countries are net financial contributors to the EU, and have been ever since the Agreement came into force in 1994. Norway, as the largest economy, pays the most, currently around 230 million Euros a year. Its annual contribution went up tenfold on enlargement of the EU, supposedly by agreement. In practice the increase was non-negotiable. The EU unilaterally declared this was the higher price that had to be paid given the ten new Member States were so poor. Norway's net contribution is now at least as large as their similar-sized neighbour Denmark – and Denmark is a full EU member.

The EU is the EEA's most important trading partner. Over 50% of Iceland's exports are to the EU, which in turn supplies nearly 70% of its imports. The figures for Norway are around 75% and 64%. Both are proud nations, anxious to preserve the independence they each gained less than a century ago, but aware that in the real world their independence is already compromised. They need to do business with the EU, but are very clear who holds the cards and calls the shots.

It is no surprise that the Norwegian Government has twice applied for EU membership. In January 1972 it formally signed a Treaty of Accession: in September the people voted 'No' in a referendum and the idea was shelved. In March 1994 the Government signed another Accession Treaty: seven months later another Referendum again threw it out. Both votes were close, but both produced the same result. The Government of the day agreed not to raise the subject for the next ten years. That time is now up.

The mood in 2004 following EU enlargement has been different, with a slight but consistent majority in the polls in support of full membership. This is despite the fact that Norway is the richest country in Europe. It has a higher GDP per head than any EU Member, thanks to its energy supplies. Fully 50% of its exports are oil and gas, and this figure may grow further as new wells in the Barents Sea are opened up. Nonetheless there is a growing awareness that Norwegians are having to accept more and more rules affecting their everyday lives without being in a position to influence them.

There is another pressure too: Norway does not wish to be marginalised politically. Within Iceland as well there is a growing feeling that now may be the time to talk – though unless the CFP is reformed the fisheries issue may still block agreement.

For the tiny principality of Liechtenstein, with its 34,000 inhabitants and 10,000 households, the issue is different. It also has full customs and monetary union with its western neighbour Switzerland. In autumn 2004 Switzerland signed a series of Treaties to bring it closer to the EU. One was designed to facilitate cross-border travel, bringing the country to all intents and purposes within the Schengen open-border zone. Another was for the Swiss to join the EU's asylum policy. Another confirmed the country is to join the European Environment Agency. Another concerned co-operation on money-laundering and tax-evasion. Step by step Switzerland is edging towards ever closer union.

With only nine embassies/missions abroad, Liechtenstein's diplomatic and consular affairs are already managed by the Swiss in the rest of the world. Effectively its economic and political future inside or outside the EU now depends largely on whether Switzerland signs any more EU Treaties.

For Iceland and Norway, the decision depends on themselves. Do they continue to go their own ways, notionally sovereign but in reality increasingly subservient to rules made elsewhere? Or do they join the club and help write those rules?

The general judgement is that they will not stay out for ever, and that one day soon they will certainly join.

The only question is when.

CHAPTER 7

Christmas votes for Turkey

Other countries have already made the decision to join.

Romania and Bulgaria are both well advanced in negotiations, and hope to join by around 2008. Croatia has been given the green light to apply. Moldova and Ukraine are expressing active interest, assuming the EU can stretch to the Urals.

How far should it stretch? Should it stretch to Turkey? That is the key question.

But what is the answer?

Officially only 3% of Turkey territory is within continental Europe. But 11% of the Turkish population live there, based around the economic and cultural capital of Istanbul, formerly Constantinople. Turks entered Anatolia in the eleventh century, finally conquering Constantinople in 1453. For centuries it has been part of the Turkish heritage, and of the European.

Our very own Father Christmas, Saint Nicholas, was Bishop of Myrna in the time of Emperor Diocletian. Noah's Ark found its final resting place on Mount Arafat. Saint Peter preached in Antioch to the first Christian community there. And Tarsus was the birthplace of Saint Paul, who made his first visit as a missionary to Anatolia.

In more recent times, Turkey joined NATO 50 years ago, binding itself to the defence of its new Western allies. It also acceded to the Organisation of European Economic Co-operation (OECD), the Conference on Security & Co-operation (OCSE) and the European Bank for Reconstruction & Development (EBRD) and the Council of Europe.

It is a full member of every major Europe-wide institution – except the European Union.

It has been already 40 years since Turkey first signed a special Association Agreement with what was then called the European Economic Community (EEC). Much water has flowed through the Bosporus since then.

In 1987, the Turkish Government formally applied to become a full Member of the European Union but its application was turned down. The arguments against were simple: the EU was a community of values including liberty, democracy, the rule of law and respect for human rights. Turkey's values were different. It was not a proper democracy given the level of political power wielded by the military; its track record in human rights was appalling, making regular use of torture and the death penalty; its record with Kurds and alleged Armenian genocide was notorious; it did not have a free market economy, and there was no freedom of the press or remotely equal rights for women. All this would have to change.

Until it did, Turks would be able to die for us as full members of NATO but never to live with us as full members of the EU.

However in 2002 the Government changed. Recep Tayyip Erdogan became Prime Minister. With the first substantial majority in the Parliament for many decades, he embarked on a programme of reform at a hectic pace.

The death penalty has been abolished. Safeguards against torture and ill-treatment have been installed. The prison system has been completely overhauled. Laws costing journalists their freedom have been repealed. The State Security Courts that condoned human rights violations have been abolished. Judgements by the European Court of Human Rights are now accepted as having supremacy over national laws. Public administration has been streamlined, Gender equality rights have been recognised and religious rights and freedoms accepted. Full Parliamentary control over military spending has been secured. The lifting of the State of Emergency in the South east of the country has led to a significant improvement in the quality of life for the Kurds. The fact that they can now produce and listen to broadcasts in their own language would have been unthinkable a mere few years ago.

All this has come from the desire to join the EU, and the realisation that Membership would not be possible without change. Conversely, without the prospect of EU Membership there would have been less pressure for change. Turkey would have stayed stuck in the past.

Instead, the country has declared its commitment to the future thanks to the European Union. The results of Erdogan's actions are already paying off. Just before Christmas 2004 the European Parliament finally voted by a large majority to give Turkey a firm and early date for the start of formal accession talks that could lead to EU membership in about ten years time.

This was followed by a unanimous decision by the European Council, with all 25 existing Member States signifying official support.

But there remain real reasons for concern. Turkey is a poor country, with an average per capita income at the levels of Bulgaria and Romania, only a quarter of the EU15 average. With a population of some 70 million, it is nearly as large as Germany. With its high birth-rate it could easily become the largest in ten years' time with well over 100 million people. In terms of influence within an enlarged EU, it would have more votes than any existing Member. The whole balance of power would shift East.

As the poorest country it would also absorb most of the available EU funds. In fact it would take many more billions than the EU currently has available. It would break the bank unless the rules changed. The good news is that Turkish entry would ensure the rules would have to be changed.

That is exactly what some people are afraid of.

French ex-President Valery Giscard d'Estaing is fiercely against Turkish membership because he regards it as an Anglo-Saxon plot to dismantle a One-Size-Fits-All Europe and reducing it to a mere trading bloc. He could well have a case.

He also fears an Islamic invasion, with 100 million Muslims joining with the 15 million already inside Europe to overwhelm its culture. Many consider the EU is and should remain a white Christian club. However the world has moved on.

Turkey has much to offer the European Union. Its geographic position alone is of vital strategic importance, having borders with Syria, Iraq and Iran. Uniquely, it straddles the critical crossroads of the Balkans, the South Caucasus and Central Asia as well as the Middle East. Since the Caspian basin has become a major source of oil and gas, the construction of the new Baku-Tbilisi-Ceyhan oil pipeline gives Turkey a key role as a transit country for vital energy supplies. The country is also a significant player in the key area of water supplies to nearby Middle Eastern countries, an issue of huge political influence for obvious reasons.

The inclusion of Turkey as a full Member State could also bring unity to the divided island of Cyprus. Without revisiting history and apportioning blame, the reality today is this beautiful island remains divided. A Green Line through Nicosia splits it in two. The people want to unite, but the politicians cannot lose face. If Turkey joins Greece inside the same club, the people's will should prevail.

Meanwhile, Turkey is a major business opportunity in its own right. Her economy is growing fast, and Foreign Direct Investment is increasing. Consumer demand will multiply as further reforms strike home. To take but one example, only a third of a million new cars were bought in Turkey in 2003, a fraction of the levels within developed EU countries. With 70-plus million consumers, the only way the market will go is up.

But above all, Europe needs Turkey as a stable, secular and democratic partner to tackle the many challenges to the East. Turkey needs Europe to underpin its drive to become a modern country anchored to the West.

The motto of the European Union is Unity in Diversity. Many feel that thus far there has been too much imposed unity and not enough real diversity. Turkey's continued exclusion would continue the problem: it could also stoke up anti-western feeling on our doorstep and inflame the fires of Islamic fundamentalism.

On the other hand, Turkey's entry could dilute the powers of Germany and France, force a radical overhaul of the

Common Agricultural Policy in particular and the EU budget in general, create new job opportunities as the Single Market expands while stimulating the values of secular democracy as an example for other Muslim states.

That is why Conservatives welcome the agreement to let negotiations begin, and voted to help them on their way.

It would be bizarre if, having successfully promoted the more diverse Europe we have long desired, the UK were promptly to leave. Fortunately it will not happen.

Politicians may be foolish, but not many of them are that foolish.

But I do know a few.

CHAPTER 8

Playing to the Gallery

Talking of these few, it is salutary to look at their recent record as MEPs.

The European Parliament voted in December 2004 to accept Turkey as a candidate country for EU membership by secret ballot. So nobody knew for certain which way different political parties voted.

That was not the case for the ten new countries that joined in May. After each Government had concluded its separate negotiations, most received resounding endorsement by their voters in separate national referenda. To complete the official process there had to be a formal vote in the European Parliament – which should indeed have been a formality. This vote was not secret, so the result was known: UKIP MEPs voted against in each case.

It may seem odd that a party that claims to champion democracy for its own country should so blatantly wish to deny it to all others. The reason presumably was that UKIP's determination to leave the EU is matched by an equal determination to see that nobody else can join – even if these people have voted overwhelmingly in favour. This is fascism, not freedom.

In summer 2004 when there was a major vote condemning human rights abuses in Darfur and for the first time labelling the atrocities as genocide, there was widespread cross-party support among MEPs from all countries. This was so important, in order to give the strongest possible signal to the Sudanese Government that the whole Parliament knew who was responsible, that we cared, and that we were not going to let the issue pass us by.

UKIP MEPs abstained.

What have been the other 'achievements' of these UKIP MEPs? Judging by the headlines back home there were two major ones in 2004 alone.

The first was when they tabled a Motion of Censure against the Commission for allowing alleged frauds within Eurostat, the EU statistical arm. It appeared that various contracts had been awarded at inflated prices to certain Commission cronies, that dummy accounts had been set up and that considerable sums could not be accounted for. The Parliament as a whole condemned what had taken place, and had ensured that the auditors were actively on the case. But UKIP got the press headlines, mainly because of their spin that Conservative MEPs had not joined them as a block in support because Conservatives didn't really care about fraud.

Given our track record in leading the clean-up this was clearly nonsense. But it made a good story.

The fact was that their Motion of Censure, if carried, would have meant the entire Commission would have gone, including the ten Commissioners from the new Member States who had been in post for all of 24 hours and had had nothing to do with the issue. The Commissioner nominally responsible, the Spanish Socialist Solbes Mira, had already left to join the new national Government in his home country. To condemn everyone else who was still there was totally inappropriate. It was also politically inept, as there would therefore be limited support among other MEPs which meant that the Censure Motion would not be carried. By tabling it, and then having it outvoted, UKIP would ensure that the Commission would appear to be cleared – the worst possible cock-up.

UKIP either didn't see this or, more likely, did not care. They believed they had a good story and were sticking to it.

Meanwhile the Conservatives drafted a different Motion, critical of those responsible, laying down a series of specific action points that should be followed, and flagging the Parliament's role as watchdog to make sure they happened. We secured widespread cross-party support for this much better Motion, and put the Commission on notice they had to sort the matter out.

Within the European Parliament, MEPs from other political parties congratulated the UK Conservative leadership on building such a strong consensus for such a positive result. The only press to mention the subject back home congratulated UKIP on taking such a splendid stand. Certain of the media had its own agenda.

The Leader of the UKIP MEPs, Nigel Farage, then gained further headlines at the time of the vote to approve the new Commission in autumn 2004, when he suddenly announced in the Parliament that the French nominee had a criminal conviction for malpractice that had not been publicly declared. Technically he was correct, in that Jacques Barrot as Secretary-General of his political party had been indicted as ultimately responsible for some funny business that had happened at lower levels. However the conviction had been covered by a general amnesty from the President before Barrot could appeal and so the slate had been wiped clean. There was therefore no criminal conviction to be declared.

Had UKIP been seriously concerned about the issue, their MEPs could have raised it at the formal Commissioner hearing just a few weeks earlier. They said nothing.

Indeed UKIP asked no questions of any kind at these hearings.

But then they are not there to engage in the issues, to achieve or to campaign for their country. Their only concern is anti-EU headlines. Or, in Kilroy's case, any headlines.

Unfortunately the main concern of certain newspapers is to provide them.

CHAPTER 9

An Australian Agenda?

The UK newspaper that provides the most consistent anti-EU headlines is the *Sun*.

Every straight banana story gets inflated coverage. Every opportunity to claim that MEPs do nothing other than draw inflated expenses is paraded. Even the issue of the European Parliament meeting in Strasbourg as well as Brussels, a dotty decision enshrined in EU Treaties years ago and requiring unanimity amongst all Member States to unscramble, was highlighted on several pages in 2004 as being suddenly 'exposed' by the paper. As intended no doubt, it generated a flurry of letters citing this waste and efficiency as proof the UK should get out of the EU.

There is no mention of anything positive ever being achieved as a result of Member States working together within the EU. There is no admission that much of the intrusive EU social legislation is actually driven by UK Labour MEPs rather than the European Commission. There is seldom any suggestion that our own Labour Government could be at fault for allowing it to happen. The cause of every perceived problem is always 'Brussels'.

There was a perfect example on 28 May 2004, just before the European Parliament elections:

> "Before you cast your vote in the European elections – if you can be bothered – consider this: thanks to the EU, dog owners will no longer be able to pick up a bone at the butcher's... Why? What the hell has this got to do with anyone in Brussels? Haven't they go enough to do, what with fiddling their expenses?... This is the reality of the EU. It is now illegal to give a dog a bone. You couldn't make it up".

So the *Sun* made it up instead.

On 13 January 2005 there was a new headline: 'The Sun launches war on Euro wasters'. It triumphantly announced the opening of a dedicated office in Brussels. Not, apparently, to understand and report EU affairs more accurately. It was specifically "to expose the waste, greed, corruption and hypocrisy at the heart of the EU." It added: "papers have been reporting from Brussels for years but most refuse to tell the real stories. Now the *Sun* will tell you what you need to know." The *Sun* of course has already decided what that is.

The *Sun* is owned by Rupert Murdoch. It is very curious that an Australian tycoon should be so deliberately negative about the EU, and apparently care so much about whether the UK is or is not a member. Or perhaps it might not be so curious after all.

One of Mr Murdoch's group of companies, BSkyB, is the EU's largest investor in interactive TV technology. Even the BBC is now starting to explore this area, with the famous 'red button' on display during the screening of the Olympics so that digital viewers could choose for themselves which sport to watch in more detail.

Murdoch has invested nearly four billion US dollars into this technology, which is currently used by some seven million homes in the UK. Much of this money would clearly be wasted if the technology suddenly changed. It could be changed at a stroke by EU politicians agreeing a new standard across all Member States.

Different media companies naturally prefer to have their own unique software in their own 'digiboxes'. That way they can control their own systems and their own network and lock competitors out.

The Commission has therefore been exploring the idea of establishing a single EU-wide operating standard, which would enable any programme to work via any 'digibox'. If this were to be imposed throughout the EU then the millions of existing set-top boxes would all have to be destroyed, and the investment written off.

Mr Murdoch might not think this a very good idea.

The good news as far as BSkyB is concerned is that the new European Commission does not think this is necessarily a good idea either. It accepts it could be unfair to penalise the companies that have already invested in their own systems, and potentially hurt the development of the Single Market. It has therefore ruled out the imposition of any central standard – for the time being.

But the Commissioner responsible has said that he will start encouraging voluntary moves towards such a single standard: he will be monitoring the extent to which broadcasters and production companies are shut out of existing systems, and he will review the situation again in 2005.

Meanwhile there are possibilities of other EU rulings, limiting the share of any media that can be held by any single media-owner.

On this basis, it could be suggested that Mr Murdoch could have compelling business reasons for hoping the EU is never strong enough to impose rules that restrict his business interests. This could be considered as one explanation why his newspapers take such a negative line towards the EU.

You might well think that – but I could not possibly comment.

CHAPTER 10

A Disunited Kingdom?

UKIP's central message is that it wants to take the United Kingdom out of the EU. I suspect this could never be done: the UK would break apart in the attempt.

In the European Parliament elections of 2004 UKIP polled 2.6 million votes, 16.2% of votes cast. It gained in every English region except the North East: with only three seats available it is less than half the size of any other region.

But it gained no seats in Wales, polling just 10.5% compared with 17.4% for Plaid Cymru.

It gained no seats in Scotland, despite seven being available. Here it polled a meagre 6.7%, just one third the level of the Scottish Nationalist Party (SNP) and well below Labour and Liberal Democrats. Even the Conservatives, not currently shining in Scotland, got nearly three times the UKIP vote.

UKIP claims the UK is currently forced to follow rules made elsewhere and promises freedom. The SNP and

Plaid Cymru claim that Scotland and Wales also have to follow rules made elsewhere. They too promise freedom: but unlike UKIP they conclude that more control from Westminster is the problem rather than the solution. They believe EU membership enhances freedom for the Scots and the Welsh rather than reduces it.

The SNP is already the second largest party in Scotland, and therefore the official Opposition in the Scottish Parliament. It wants independence for its country. Its website gives the reasons: "Independence would mean decisions about tax, about social security benefits and about investment in our public services, about defence, about broadcasting and a whole range of other issues would be taken by people who live here and not by remote politicians in Westminster". UKIP might agree with that – except that it would replace the word Westminster with Brussels.

But the SNP labels itself as a Pro-European party. It wants to be "an independent nation in the mainstream of modern Europe". Eleven of the current 25 EU Member States are the same size or smaller than Scotland. All have their independent voice. Scotland wants to stay in the EU, but as a country at the top table and not a mere region of the UK.

Plaid Cymru's vision is for "an independent Wales playing a progressive and radical role in the EU". It too wants to free itself from the shackles of Westminster control. It does not see Welsh independence in any way being diluted by being part of the EU. In fact it sees the opposite:

"An independent Wales would be on an equal footing with other small countries – with more seats in the European Parliament, full voting rights in the Council of Ministers, and representation in the (European) Commission.... Plaid Cymru sees Europe as an increasingly important player that can truly represent our interests globally."

The fact that the Welsh represent only half of one per cent of the total EU population makes them realise that the country would be inaudible on its own. With her own voice in Europe Wales could at last be heard.

The fact that Wales will have received about £1.5billion of EU funds in the 2000-2006 spending round may possibly have helped promote their passion. No party in Wales could put such funding at risk.

Suppose UKIP succeeded in holding a referendum on UK membership of the European Union, and then succeeded in getting a 'No' vote. Would it not be likely that a clear majority in Wales and Scotland would vote the other way? What then? Would the votes of an English majority to pull out of the EU be passively accepted in Wales and Scotland? Welsh and Scottish voters from all major political parties see membership of the EU as a strength. They would not acquiesce quietly in exchanging this for weakness outside, especially if they were still run by Westminster.

A referendum vote for the whole UK to leave the EU would not lead to the whole UK leaving. It would be much more likely to lead to Wales and Scotland clamouring for separate Referenda to leave the UK, and maybe even a new barrier going up between Northern Ireland and the Republic. England would be going it alone, with the United Kingdom becoming Disunited.

We should be trying to make the UK stronger, not pushing to break it apart.

The point is that the whole UKIP message is phoney. It is not a UK party. It may care passionately about the future of its country, but its country is England. It is an English party, not battling for Great Britain but for Little England.

Of course it could not possibly admit it.

Anyway, EIP does not quite have the same resonance as UKIP.

CHAPTER 11

Flemings and Lemmings

Within the EU there are other political parties also pushing for independence. One of the most prominent is in Belgium, where the Vlaams Blok wants Flanders to split from Wallonia and nuzzle up to the Netherlands.

In the June 2004 regional elections it secured nearly a quarter of the popular vote within Flanders. But that did not stop it being declared a criminal organisation by the Belgian Supreme Court for its extreme racist views.

The Vlaams Blok rejects all ideas of a multicultural society as being 'erroneous'. A centrepiece of its manifesto is the preservation of the cultural identity of the Flemish people, which includes the forcible deportation of all "aliens and immigrants" who do not conform completely with Flemish values and habits.

The people who seem to be regarded as the most alien of all are their neighbours within Belgium, the Walloons. Not only do the Walloons speak French rather than Flemish, a major sin in itself: they are also (according to the Blok) benefiting from an unfair share of overall Belgian wealth and national income. This is a problem.

The Blok's solution is to break up Belgium.

One of their minor challenges is what to do with Brussels. The capital of Flanders (as well as of Belgium), it is a French-speaking island surrounded by Flemish-speakers. The master-plan would be to include Brussels within the breakaway State. This doesn't seem to generate too many votes in Brussels.

Belgium is indeed a somewhat artificial construction, but it works. It has worked since it was formally constituted only as recently as 1831, when it was set up as a separate and independent country by the Great Powers of the day – including Great Britain. The intention was in part to limit the powers of the Netherlands by preventing them grabbing one half of the territory and in part to rein back France who wanted to grab the other half. This has worked too.

Breaking up Belgium might solve one small problem, but would create bigger ones.

Breaking up the EU would do the same.

Protesting has its price.

CHAPTER 12

The Voice of America

It has been suggested that the UK should leave the EU and instead join NAFTA (the North Atlantic Free Trade Association).

America wants us to be in the European Union.

The fact is that the USA's most important trading partner is not NAFTA but the EU, and this importance has mounted as the years have gone by.

In the 1950's, Europe accounted for merely 20% of American global investment. In the 60's it had doubled to 40%. In the 70's it was over 45%, and in the 80's and 90's over 50%. By the turn of the century Europe accounted for well over 60% of American investment outflows, as a direct result of increasing market liberalisation within the European Single Market. US companies now rely on the European Union for roughly half their annual foreign profits.

American investment has reached every EU country, but

one country has received more than most of the others put together. For corporate America the most important market in the world is the UK. In 2001 US assets in the UK were worth $1.4 trillion, as much as Asia, Latin America, Africa and the Middle East combined. Over 15% of total UK exports are now accounted for by American-owned companies.

This has occurred for many reasons. We speak the same language, we share similar beliefs regarding free trade, and we have relatively flexible labour markets compared to our continental European colleagues. All these combine to make the UK an ideal place for US manufacturers and service providers to locate as the main EU gateway through which their goods can enter the Single European Market.

If the UK was no longer a member of the EU, that gateway would be shut. American companies would have to find another door.

US businesses welcome an EU that is strong. It is so much easier for them to do business with one large block – and the larger the better – especially when such a block increasingly has just one set of rules to follow. It also saves negotiating 25 separate sets of bilateral trade agreements.

The increasing importance of the EU as a market for US goods is simply shown by looking at the Commercial section of the US Embassy in Brussels. Ten years ago there were just two people. Today there are 14.

Meanwhile, the largest potential market in the world is China. A recent survey (Partners in Prosperity, by Daniel S. Hamilton and Joseph P. Quinlan) has observed that "Central and Eastern Europe's inexpensive yet skilled labour force, along with its proximity to – and now membership of – the European Union, makes the region an ideal export platform to one of the largest markets in the world."

This could be a major problem for us. The UK is the current favoured gateway for US companies, by virtue of its membership of the EU and for the other reasons listed earlier. But Central and Eastern Europe are on standby with a much cheaper gateway, much closer to Asian markets.

As one US Company Chief Executive said to me very simply, in response to my query whether our withdrawal from the EU would change his commitment to the UK: "it would change everything".

US companies currently employ 1.1 million people inside the UK. These jobs are not guaranteed to stay. If the UK left the EU, they might well leave too. Such jobs would go East.

But Americans are concerned with the UK and Europe not just for business reasons. The politics are important too. US politicians are very aware of the French agenda aimed at setting up a competitor to America – not just in terms of economic might but also as a political and 'moral' counterweight as well. Only the active presence of the United Kingdom as an EU Member will ensure that the principle of atlanticism is promoted within Europe, with America being seen as a strong political ally.

Margaret Thatcher made this clear back in 1990 in a famous speech to the Aspen Institute in Colorado entitled: 'Shaping a new Global Community':

"Britain's destiny lies in Europe as a full member of the Community. We shall not be standing on the sidelines or, as you would say, watching from the bleachers. On the contrary, we shall bring it to our own distinctive point of view – practical and down to earth. We fight hard for what we believe in, namely: a Europe based on willing co-operation between independent sovereign states; a Europe which is an expression of economic freedom, without which political freedom could not long endure; a Europe which does not resort to protectionism, but remains open to the outside world; and – of supreme importance to Britain – a Europe which always seeks the closest possible partnership with the United States".

This is of supreme importance to America too. The EU is not just a trading opportunity: it is also a major political project.

CHAPTER 13

A Political Project

Many people thought they had just joined a Common Market back in 1973.

The Christopher Booker/Richard North book *The Great Deception* maintains this was a con at the time, that there was always a cunning plan to turn Europe into a single Superstate, that every separate EU development over the past fifty years has been carefully choreographed to this end.

Quite why so many democratically elected Governments should have been conniving in such a plan is never explained. Quite how so many millions of people have apparently been bamboozled into voting 'Yes' in referenda throughout the ten new Member States is never addressed. Quite why there are still new countries queuing to join is never even raised.

The EU has certainly evolved politically, but in ways that were never foreseen. The fall of the Berlin Wall in 1989, the collapse of the Soviet Union, the progressive democratisation of their former satellite states – all were hoped for in the distant future but none were expected so suddenly. Such events confirm that the simple Common Market has indeed moved on, that there is now a very clear political agenda.

As Margaret Thatcher said in a speech to the Hoover Institution in Washington back in 1991: "The European Community does indeed have a political mission. It is to anchor new and vulnerable democracies more securely to freedom and to the West."

To this day this remains a key mission for our continent, and it is important for the UK to help shape it.

This means staying at the continental Top Table.

Such a political mission is not completely new. In fact the original mission of the EU was also primarily political, to secure peace in Europe. "If trade cannot cross borders, soldiers will." By effectively removing borders and trade barriers, mutual trade would bind countries together. The Common Market was not just an end in itself, but seen as a means to secure that end.

In the words of Robert Schuman, the intention was to make war "not just unthinkable, but materially impossible".

It was not NATO that would secure peace within Europe: NATO's role was to see off threats from outside. It was inside where the historic problem lay, and where a new solution was needed. The solution proposed was that people, goods, money and services should be able to move freely within a single community.

It was about living together as well as trading together. It was never just about trade on its own. It was about a structure for Europe's future, to ensure the savagery and inhumanity of the past could never again contaminate the present.

For centuries the continent of Europe has suffered wars consuming entire generations. It has seen communism, gulags, concentration camps, secret police, fascism and the attempt to wipe out the entire Jewish race – all very much within living memory.

Europe has yearned for a different vision, a vision of shared values, a vision that put the freedoms of people ahead of the perversions of political leaders.

To say today that this vision is now yesterday's agenda, that we have had peace for 50-plus years so we don't need the EU anymore, misses the point entirely. We still need a political structure permanently in place which allows us to discuss our ongoing differences openly and to resolve them peaceably. We need a structure that will prevent Germany, as the largest European country and with its capital at Europe's geographical centre, from ever dominating its neighbours in future. This is what the EU aims to provide.

We also need a structure that is stronger than the sum of

its parts. If individual countries are to agree to share their sovereignty in certain areas, they expect their influence to be increased and not diluted. There is plenty of evidence to show how important this is in an increasingly globalised world.

When President George W. Bush imposed sanctions on imports of steel into the US as a protectionist measure to help his uncompetitive domestic steel industry the EU was swift to retaliate. It produced a long list of US-made products which would have high duties slapped upon them on entering the European Union unless America climbed down by a certain date.

Virtually the very day the deadline expired the President lifted his sanctions on steel. His argument back home was that the duration of the sanctions had been sufficient to help domestic producers recover, and that sanctions were now no longer required.

Their removal was of course nothing to do with the reciprocal threat from the EU.

The timing was of course complete co-incidence.

Nobody really believed this.

If the EU did not exist, and instead there had been 25 separate 'sovereign' countries all separately complaining to the United States, there is little doubt that the President would have felt no pressure.

Only if you have real weight are you in a position to throw it around. Sovereignty should mean power: sometimes you have to pool it in order to achieve it.

The EU has collectively spoken out against human rights abuses in Darfur. It has led the campaign for a re-run of the fraudulent Presidential election in Ukraine. It has been single-minded in its condemnation of the Mugabe regime in Zimbabwe, and imposed an EU-wide travel ban on its leaders.

It does not always speak with one voice. France's determination to oppose America over Iraq, announcing it would veto any second UN Resolution whatever it would say, led to deep divisions within Europe. But at least such divergence of views shows democracy is still alive and well in the EU, that conformity in foreign policy is not compulsory – at least this side of the proposed EU Constitution.

But when all Member States do choose to support each other, the impact can be immediate. The UK felt this at first hand during the campaign to restore freedom to the Falkland Islands. We did not just rely on Ronald Reagan, who was initially noticeably backward in coming forward. We called for support from our European friends.

In opening the debate in the House of Commons in April 1982, Prime Minister Thatcher was able to boast: "We have been urging our friends and allies to take action parallel to our own, and we have achieved a heartening degree of success. The most significant measure has been the decision of our (then) eight partners in the European Community to join us not just in an arms embargo but also in stopping all imports from Argentina. This is a very important step, unprecedented in its scope and the rapidity of the decision."

The EU gives us not just trading colleagues but political partners too – in Europe as well as America.

CHAPTER 14

The Glory that was France

Some people believe that EU rules were mainly made by the French for the French.

That was certainly the original idea when the EU began. In her thirst for *La Gloire*, France realised after the War that she could never be Top Nation on her own. But as a senior member of a community of nations crafted in her image she could conceivably lay claim to such a role. And for many years she did precisely that, which was very smart – with Germany paying through the nose for the privilege which was even smarter.

Keeping Britain out helped enormously.

But once the UK was allowed inside 'her' cosy club, all this would change. The French now consider *Les Anglo-Saxons* to be finally and firmly in charge. Now would be a dotty time for the Brits to leave.

It is worth remembering how things used to be. Of the six original EU founder members, three were French: France, Belgium and Luxembourg. The three official seats of the European Parliament were all francophone: Strasbourg, Brussels and Luxembourg. Everything about them was French. But progressively with each successive EU enlargement the French influence has diluted, so much so that an extraordinary document was presented to the French National Assembly in May 2004.

It is 71 pages of long lament.

Its opening headline admits "the end of The Golden Age of French presence". It chronicles how France left its imprint on the construction of Europe in three key areas: political, in the establishment of the way of working known as *la méthode communautaire*, and in the provision of six of the 25 Presidents of the Parliament; administrative, in the provision of the rules of procedure and the organisation of the European Court; linguistic, in the leadership of the French language and the location of the institutions in French or French-speaking cities.

That is now history.

The Parliament and its Committees are now effectively run, and indeed run effectively, by the Germans and the British.

The French language is on the slide. In olden days, English might have been already the language of business but French was regarded (at least by the French) as the language of diplomacy. When it was the turn of Africa to produce the new Secretary-General of the United Nations, France objected to Kofi Annan because he was not from French Africa.

Kofi still got the job.

As recently as 1997, more documents were prepared for the European Council in French than in any other language. A mere five years later, 73% were prepared in English with only 18% in French.

The official welcome page on the website of the European Central Bank is in English: if you click on the icon for the French language you are politely told that currently all key information is only available in English.

Finally, a survey of the political elite of Eastern Europe shows that 62% speak English, 48% speak German, and only 7% admit to speaking French.

By their own admission in this same document, the French are seen as the bad boys of Europe. Not only is France one of the worst at transposing EU laws into French national legislation, and then one of the worst at obeying them: French MEPs are seen as relative part-timers, allowing the more active British to make more waves.

In terms of positions of power in the various Directorate-Generalships, France is now behind Italy and Germany as well as the UK.

In terms of *le lobbying*, given that Brussels is now the world capital with more than 10,000 lobbyists, France also scores badly. When it comes to the number of national media representatives accredited, France ranks a lowly number five.

The analysis admits that the national Government is seen as 'arrogant', and professes no surprise that incoming Commission President Barroso has allotted the junior portfolio of Transport to the French Commissioner nominee Jacques Barrot. How are the mighty fallen.

It is a remarkable document.

It offers no remedy. It acknowledges that the damage is a fait accompli. It is a testimony to the slow persistence of the British in the years since we have joined, and a reminder of what we have achieved.

France has yet to come to terms with this new political reality. Her influence will be further diluted as a result of EU enlargement, with new entrants being more economically liberal as well as more English-speaking. Pascal Lamy, the French former Commissioner for Trade, has acknowledged that "the French have to realise that Europe will be something different from a big France".

If President Chirac realises it, he is not admitting it. He maintains, at least in public, that the tide can be reversed. He is offering free French language lessons to the new entrants, so that they can feel familiar with French. He is pushing for other Member States to raise their taxes so that France will not have to reduce hers. He is trying to develop a triangular axis with Spain and Germany in the fading months of Gerhardt Schroeder's Chancellorship, to pretend there is a 'multi-polar' world with several key players rather than a uni-polar concept of America run by George Bush.

Chirac has no chance whatever of success in this game – unless we help him by leaving the field.

CHAPTER 15

Metric Matters

One area where France did succeed in championing change was the introduction of the metric system. This was brought in by the French during the rule of Napoleon Bonaparte – which could explain why the British have resisted it for so long.

The Paris Academy of Sciences formally proposed the system to the French National Assembly back in 1791. Impeccable Gallic logic argued that the basic unit of measurement, to be called the metre, should be defined as one ten-millionth of a meridianal quadrant of the earth. The idea was slow to catch on even in France, but it finally gained momentum after it was made mandatory in 1840. In 1875 an international treaty was signed to create an International Bureau of Weights and Measures to ensure the metric system became the global standard.

The Bureau would be based in Paris.

For some people back in Britain the imposition of an alien

system of standardised weights and measures, especially a French system, was and is an attack on our very way of life. We may have lost our empire, but to lose our imperial weights and measures is one diktat from Brussels that has to be resisted at all costs.

Except it hasn't come from Brussels. It has come from history, given other countries were changing. It has come from business, most of whose customers converted years ago – leaving many UK exporters at a competitive disadvantage in having to produce metric and non-metric versions of the same goods.

The 'Metric Martyrs', in opposing metrication of fruit and vegetables, and claiming to be making a stand against Brussels, were fingering the wrong enemy. Those ultimately responsible were British Governments more than a century apart.

The decision to convert to the metric system in the UK was made by an all-party Select Committee of the House of Commons way back in 1862. The logic was unarguable and the decision was unanimous. Metrication was on the march not just in Europe but throughout the world. It was time to catch the bus.

By 1864 the metric system was officially permitted for UK trade. By 1897 this was formally legalised by Parliament via the Weights and Measures Act.

Nothing to do with Brussels at all.

Despite the new Act, the Government still hesitated over scrapping imperial weights and measures, without which the metric system would never really happen. It seemed a huge step to take at the time, so although the decision remained agreed in principle no Government had the courage to implement it in practice.

Scroll forward one hundred years.

In 1965, a full eight years before the UK entered the Common Market, the Government finally took the decision to convert completely to metric over the following ten years. But they still didn't actually do it. The Minister for Metrication was Geoffrey Howe: to this day he apologetically admits his share of blame in agreeing to slow the whole process down.

It is true that there would later be an EU Directive confirming that all Member States should adopt the metric system, a Directive that the UK was happy to sign up to as long as there was permanent protection for the pint (for beer but not for milk) and the mile. But the Government then secured a special 'derogation' for ten years to keep the old imperial system of pounds and ounces alive in shops alongside the metric equivalents. This derogation was then renewed for a further ten years while the Government continued to dither.

Meanwhile other countries just got on with the job. Even former members of the British Empire such as Australia, New Zealand, India and South Africa completed their own conversion process to move away entirely from imperial measurements without deviation or hesitation.

Only one major country – albeit an important one – has yet to go fully metric and that is America. Congress passed the Metric Conversion Act in 1975 "to co-ordinate and plan the increasing use of the metric system in the United States". Currently it is still voluntary but well over a third of US companies, including the Pentagon itself, have already made the change.

It took Tony Blair, to his great credit, to decide not to renew the UK derogation and to get on with enforcing a single standard. But then to his great discredit, his Government adopted an excessively authoritarian approach in driving it forward. It decreed that anyone caught selling in imperial weights after a certain date would face a criminal prosecution leading to a punitive fine and possible jail.

This was not part of any Brussels Directive: it was a decision made in Downing Street.

It got a number of people very cross – including Brussels, which got all the blame.

Meanwhile, an enterprising pub in Worcestershire decided to sell Austrian beer – in litres. This was against the UK law and so the pub was prosecuted. Metric martyrs got yet more publicity railing against Brussels bureaucrats who had no role in the matter whatever. The Worcestershire pub of course did extra good business.

It really is time that we finally gave up our pounds and ounces, just as we gave up the Groat all those years ago – not because of any Directive but in the common cause of common sense and getting up-to-date.

Mind you, I shall personally miss the demise of the Bushel.

For the past 30 years in our schools only the metric system has been taught to our youngsters. It is time for us oldsters to change and catch up. But that means Governments giving the lead rather than cracking the whip.

However this is not the first time Britannia has been slow to embrace new rules.

When Britain converted to Celsius from Fahrenheit, voters were equally unenthusiastic. To help us, the Government decided that for many years we should use both systems. Effectively we still do. Officially we only measure temperature in Celsius/Centigrade but the TV weather forecast usually helpfully converts this back to Fahrenheit as well. The *Daily Telegraph* still gives both. So for many people, the change has yet to happen.

Only with decimal currency some 30 years ago did the change occur virtually overnight. Again some people protested, used to Pounds, Shillings and Pence. Again it was a Labour Government, this time under Harold Wilson, which decided change was necessary. Again, the change had been rather late in arriving.

By the time Britain decided to go decimal in 1969, only four other countries in the world were still using a non-decimal system.

At least one of them would have found it hard to change. Its unit of currency was the cigarette tin.

CHAPTER 16

Time is on Our Side

A century ago, France led the world into the future with its proposals for metrication. She is now trying to lead Europe back into the past with plans for a European Constitution.

Deliberately rushed through ahead of the accession of the ten new Member States, the Constitution was carefully crafted by a founder member of the *ancien régime*, Giscard d'Estaing.

It is the final fanfare of Old Europe. Its proposals would not just promote a federal Europe: they would set it in stone.

There would be a new Foreign Minister (actually called Minister, a title more usually associated with a Government) responsible for promoting a Common Foreign and Security Policy. This would not appear to be voluntary. It lays down unambiguously that: "Member States shall actively and unreservedly support the Union's common foreign and security policy in a spirit of loyalty and mutual solidarity and shall comply with the Acts adopted by the Union in this area."

There would be an EU Finance Minister, responsible for "ensuring co-ordination" of economic and employment policy throughout the Union.

The EU would be endowed with its own legal identity, able to sign Treaties on its own behalf instead of enduring the tedious process of waiting for democratically-elected Member States to sign them. As such, it could legitimately lay claim to its own seat at the United Nations, in which case it would scarcely be sensible for mere Member States in the EU to continue holding separate seats of their own.

Member States would lose their national vetoes in at least twenty new areas, with issues such as asylum and immigration moving towards Qualified Majority Voting. The European Court of Justice would be given new powers over how Member States deal with asylum seekers, including the application of social security benefits.

EU law would be given primacy over national UK law not only on Single Market issues but also in areas such as "freedom, security and justice".

Competition policy would become an exclusive competence of the EU.

The EU would gain more powers over energy policy. As the UK is the major EU producer of oil and gas this would affect us more than most. One proposed Directive alone, specifying increased statutory reserve requirements for oil, could cost the UK more than £3billion.

The EU would gain further powers to increase harmonisation of legal procedures in criminal cases. It would increasingly control the rights of criminals and how evidence could be used against them. It also would determine people's rights on arrest. The appointment of a European Public Prosecutor would signal the beginning of the end of the UK Criminal Justice system.

None of this is even a small step towards transparency, simplification and re-connecting with the people. All of this is giant leap towards greater centralisation, which must be why Labour and Liberal Democrats are so much in favour of it.

Derek Scott, former economic adviser to Tony Blair, has concluded: "It will entrench Europe's economic failings, and drag Britain down too."

Sir Digby Jones of the CBI puts it more kindly but still curtly: "It does nothing to make Europe more globally competitive."

The LibDem Spokesman Andrew Duff MEP has welcomed it with effusive enthusiasm. He commented: "It is the optimum solution at this stage of European integration". Well, I suppose if it is European integration you are actually after, then it is indeed the optimum solution.

When Kilroy-Silk was asked by the *Yorkshire Post* for his personal analysis of the proposals he replied: "I have got more important things to do than spend my time reading a boring subject like the European Constitution".

By more important things, perhaps he meant fighting for the leadership of his party? Much more important than actually fighting for his country.

He admitted he hadn't even bothered to read it. He was later to brand his UKIP colleagues as 'lazy', and leave the party altogether.

A Foreign & Commonwealth Office press release claims that signing up to the Constitution is somehow "central to the Government's belief that the UK should remain a strong and influential power in a peaceful, effective and flexible Europe".

Maybe the Government hasn't read it either.

The Trade Unions have certainly read it.

In fact they wrote a fair chunk of it, specifically the Charter of Fundamental Rights.

The TUC website has given its own observations on the Charter: "There is a general consensus that perhaps the most important quality of the EU Charter is that it breaks new ground by including in a single list of fundamental rights not only traditional civil and political rights, but also a long list of social and economic rights. The EU Charter included provisions, among them fundamental trade union rights, which are at the heart of labour law in Europe...The incorporation of the EU Charter into the primary constitutional law of the EU will have an impact on the Member States, bound by the Charter through the doctrine of supremacy of EU law."

It is no wonder the Trade Unions quite like it. They are also delighted that "for the first time the EU will be able to pass laws protecting the public sector".

The only perceived drawback they highlight is that "the drive towards removing barriers to trade in goods and services, the development of the internal market and the removal of state subsidies is maintained (although not increased) in the Treaty."

It is no wonder that the Left are now pro-EU. It is they who have been setting the agenda: this Treaty would be their triumph.

It is also no wonder that *The Economist* front cover for June 21st 2003 had a picture of a dustbin. Its headline was: 'Where to file Europe's new Constitution.'

Derek Scott concluded his remarks on the Constitution as follows: "Only in Britain is the Government presenting the argument in terms of 'in or out' of Europe... Most of those opposed to the Constitution are not saying 'Scrap the EU'. They are calling for a political structure that is more in tune with the aspirations of Europe's peoples and less designed to meet the inclinations and ambitions of its politicians and bureaucrats.... In any case there has to be another Treaty when Romania and Bulgaria join in 2008/9.

Provided the Constitution is rejected, time is on our side."

We must use that time.

Conservatives have committed to hold a referendum in autumn 2005 if we win a May General Election. Given the UK holds the six-month Presidency of the European Council in the second half of the year, this timing would maximise our leverage to drive change. We shall campaign for a 'No' vote.

If the 'No' vote wins the day in the UK, as seems likely, certain other EU countries may press ahead on their own towards greater political integration. That is their right. But we shall have established the clear principle that One-Size-Fits-All EU policies for every single issue will no longer apply. Britannia has rights too.

The UK is not compelled to ratify the Constitution. Others may if they wish.

Tony Blair clearly does wish to. Given the damage it would do to the country this is most curious. There must be a special reason. One wonders what it might be.

Certainly the Constitution calls for a full-time President of the Council. The job would become vacant in 2006/7.

The ideal candidate would be a world statesman, preferably an EU Member State Prime Minister who had decided to stand down round about then.

Tony Blair is so unusually keen on this Constitution that I do hope he has a good candidate in mind.

CHAPTER 17

The New Battlegrounds

The fights within Europe today are not on traditional battlefields, and people are no longer exhorted – or compelled – to lay down their lives in the process.

But there are real fights nonetheless, on issues of supreme importance regarding the future of the EU in general and as to who rules Britannia in particular.

The proposed Constitution is by far the biggest battleground, but there are others.

There is the whole issue of Commission reform. The fact that the EU accounts have not been formally signed off by the EU Court of Auditors for ten successive years is not just a disgrace. It is an outrage. Back in 2002 Marta Andreasen, the newly appointed Commission Chief Accountant employed to sort out the mess, highlighted the basic failings of the Commission accounting system. The National Audit Office had established that in 2002 alone there were 10,000 examples of possible fraud in the accounts. She admitted publicly that the system was still wide open to fraud, because too many people could access it and make changes without being specifically authorised. She pleaded for support. The response was her immediate suspension by the Commission Vice-President for Reform, our very own Neil Kinnock. Just days before he was due to step down, Commissioner Kinnock converted the suspension into full dismissal – while he then went on to the House of Lords. Her offence? To blow the whistle on the problem publicly instead of hiding it.

The whole credibility of the EU is laid on the line by such a sequence of actions. We need a proper accounting system – and we need a proper Commissioner responsible who will fight to secure it.

We also need a system whereby whistle-blowers are applauded rather than fired.

Above all, we need a culture of responsibility amongst all the officials, with awareness at all levels that the Commission is the servant of the people and not the master.

Finally, we also need to reduce the potential for fraud and mismanagement in the first place.

Over 90% of the budget is spent within Member States, yet Member State Governments are not officially responsible. They should be. Where the money is managed is where it should be controlled. Better still, much of the money should never go into the EU budget to begin with but should stay with Member States. In addition, the European Parliament should recognise its own responsibility as a guardian of the budget and stop coming up with more and more proposals to increase it for pet projects. Socialist MEPs are particularly prone to doing this, given their conviction they always know best how to spend other people's money.

MEPs also contribute to the problem in other ways, according to Marta Andreasen. Writing in *The Times* in December 2004, she observed:

> "The institution responsible for this state of affairs is primarily the Commission, even though in recent years this institution has reverted to blaming Member countries. But above them are the MEPs. The European Parliament's job is to shout for the taxpayer. Instead it has refused to hear me, which surprised me because I was trying to speak on behalf of the taxpayer. Worse, MEPs continue to give discharge to the Commission on its financial responsibility, in the knowledge of the vulnerability of the system to fraud and the lack of action to resolve this situation for the past ten years. The leader of the Liberal Group at the European Parliament, Graham Watson, even praised Signor Prodi for my dismissal."

As Marta knows, Conservatives voted in favour of her appearing in Committee, and against the budget discharge. We deplored her dismissal. We shall continue to campaign for these problems to be addressed, but success will elude us without the support of other political parties.

It will also elude us if Member States themselves fail to support change. The issue of budgetary management and control is a major battleground in its own right, one in which our own Government needs to be much more actively engaged.

Then there is the basic battle to complete the Common Market. The easy decisions were taken long ago. As EU citizens we can drive around freely from country to country on the continent without being held up at borders and without the need for special documents. We can buy what we like, where we like, without limit. We can move our money between countries as we wish. We can work and study, live and die, in any EU Member State.

But this is only part of the story. Many countries still try every which way to protect their own domestic markets, with hidden state aid or with cleverly crafted non-tariff barriers. These issues have to be tackled – with patience, with persistence, and above all with total commitment. As the world's greatest free trader, this is massively in our own national interest. It can only be tackled from within the EU. Conservatives are leading this battle too, and are slowly but surely making a difference.

The main battle is to free us from the shackles of socialism, the mounting burden of red tape and regulation which may start life in Brussels but grows up through adolescence into full maturity in Whitehall. This too can only be done at source, at both sources.

Finally there is the battle to determine the political future of Europe, within a changing and dangerous world. It is not a question, as one Ukipper said to me recently, of "Are you saying that Britain is not strong enough to stand on her own two feet?" We should not wish to. We have a role to play in the wider world that it is in our own national interest to play. For such a role you need to be on the same field as the other players.

We need to ensure Europe does not look inwards, but plays a part in shaping solutions in key areas of the world, of which Darfur, Kashmir and Palestine are but a few. We should expect to play a part in determining the very shape of Europe, whether Turkey should be allowed to join perhaps to be followed by a democratic Ukraine. We need to embrace the best of America, without being its poodle. We also need to enlist support for the nations of New Europe, who are as desirous of change as we are.

At the time of the European Parliamentary elections in summer 2004 there was a flurry of UKIP letters in the local press which I felt I had to show a new friend – Jacek Saryusz-Wolski MEP, Leader of the Polish MEPs from the Civic Platform Party of Poland. He was so incensed he agreed to send a letter in reply as follows:

"Your local MEP Philip Bushill-Matthews has shown me the comments from Mr Arnott of the UK Independence Party published in your newspaper comparing the EU to the Soviet Union and the NAZI occupation of Europe.

This is not just absurd. This is in an insult to the Polish people who suffered under both the NAZI and the Soviet regimes before finally regaining our freedom. As the Minister responsible over many years for negotiating Poland's accession to the European Union it is also offensive to me personally.

My country joined the EU in May, after a national referendum in which a clear majority of our people voted in favour. We did not vote to surrender our freedom again but to secure it for the future.

We voted to heal the divisions in Europe, to work constructively with our sister countries to promote a Europe of free markets and free peoples. I am proud to work alongside British Conservative MEP colleagues in the European Parliament who share the same agenda. We deplore the agenda of the UK Independence Party that would create a new division of Europe and undermine our task."

This is the biggest battle of all.

Nothing less than total victory will suffice.

It is unfortunate, to put it mildly, that Conservatives should have to fight UKIP in order to secure it.

CHAPTER 18

Absent Friends

In order to pull your weight in Europe you have to be around to pull it.

That may sound particularly obvious. It is not obvious to everybody.

Given that the main decisions in the EU are taken by the European Council, it is particularly important that senior UK Cabinet Ministers attend key meetings in order to safeguard British interests and fight our corner when necessary (which should be all of the time).

Other countries see this very clearly. The current Labour Government does not.

Out of 50 EU Foreign Affairs Council meetings between 2002 and 2004 the UK Foreign Secretary Jack Straw attended only 33. The remaining 17 were attended by junior ministers or civil servants, trying to hold their own with senior Cabinet Ministers from other countries. Jack's opposite numbers from other Member States, including

France and Germany, attend more regularly, thereby enabling their Governments to punch their full weight.

Gordon Brown's record is also poor. His attendance at EU Finance Ministers Council meetings has been declining steadily since 2002. One EU official, quoted in *The Times* on 19 November 2004, commented: "Brown doesn't really get on with any of the other ministers, and often doesn't bother showing up. We've always no idea whether he is coming."

The record shows that he also managed to get to only two-thirds of the meetings, 19 out of a possible 29.

That of course does not stop him lecturing his counterparts on what they should be doing. In mid-November 2004 he published a damning Report saying that other countries were failing to provide a level playing-field for countries such as the UK to compete for a fair share of the £1000billion of business awarded under Member States' Government contracts. In a fanfare of press publicity, he declared he would be going to the next Finance Ministers' meeting in Brussels in order so sort it – and them – out.

He did go to this particular meeting. But he did not even put the item on the agenda. He gave no copies of his Report to any other Government, and indeed made no comment about it at all. It was suggested later there were very good reasons for this. Firstly the 'facts' in the Report were largely contrived and would not bear close scrutiny. Secondly, they were not really intended to be scrutinised: they were primarily an exercise in Eurosceptic spin for UK domestic consumption ahead of an early 2005 General Election.

But Straw's and Brown's absences pale in comparison with those of David Blunkett. The EU Justice and Home Affairs Ministers' Council is particularly important. This is where the establishment of a possible European Public Prosecutor is discussed. This is where the threat to the UK Criminal Justice system is played out, with the potential replacement of Corpus Juris by the Napoleonic Code. These are issues vital to the UK national interest.

Out of 19 possible meetings, Home Secretary David Blunkett managed the grand total of four. Maybe he was too busy arranging visas.

The UK Government has also given up any attempt to control its Old Labour colleagues in the European Parliament. They allow their own Labour MEPs to follow their separate Socialist agenda rather than support the Government line. These MEPs tried to vote down the Barroso Commission despite a personal plea from the Prime Minister. They regularly call for more rights for workers, more powers for trade unions, and more burdens on business — again against the official wish of the Government whose policies they are elected to represent.

When the majority of laws affecting the UK are now initiated at EU level, one might have expected the Government to play a leading role in the EU corridors of power in challenging them. Such a role is clearly there to be played. France and Germany play it all the time.

Britannia has the authority to help shape these rules much more decisively. If her current Government Ministers have other priorities you can't blame Brussels.

CHAPTER 19

The Kommissars

The EU 'Rulebook', or *Acquis Communautaire*, is 80,000 pages long and is still growing. As a result the European Commission, as the body responsible, gets called a lot of names – not all of them printable.

Commissioners themselves have many official names, depending on which of the 20 EU languages you choose. I prefer German, as this calls them Kommissars.

To me this conjures up an image of be-ribboned dictators complete with jackboots, never listening to reason and barking out orders for the rest of us to obey. This is of course a most mischievous suggestion, though one that would be readily believed in the UK. When the Commission was originally set up, it was probably even true.

The intention always was for the Commission to be a seriously strong Executive. In the early days the European Council (made up of the Heads of Member State Governments) was expected to rely on the Commission both to set the agenda and to make it happen. At the same time the European Parliament was just a largely irrelevant talking-shop. But each successive Treaty has changed the balance of power between the various EU Institutions. The European Council is now the driving force within the EU, with the European Parliament gaining real powers of 'co-decision' alongside.

Like any Parliament, the European Parliament also has a genuine role in keeping a check on the Executive, in this case the Commission. This was made startlingly obvious to all when in November 2004 the incoming Commission President Barroso suddenly withdrew his proposed new team to make key changes. He knew a majority in the Parliament was itching to vote against the line-up approved by Member States, because of concern about the quality and the judgement of several of the nominees. Rather than face his Commission being voted down he decided to back off rapidly. He knows where the powers now lie, even if the voters have yet to catch up.

The current reality is that the Commission, which since EU enlargement consists of 25 Commissioners and their teams, actually has limited powers. When decisions are to be made, the Commission can and does make its proposals. But the Commission cannot decide. The Commission has no votes. Votes are divided between the elected European Council and the elected European Parliament, and in both institutions the British have a strong voice. We also have strong friends in both who agree with us on a regular basis.

The Commission's formal role is to act as 'Guardian of the

Treaties'. This means its duty is to come up with legislative proposals to give effect to the decisions signed up to in these Treaties by Member State Governments. So if we don't like what the Commission is doing, it is the Member States we should blame for the original decisions.

The Commission can push for acceptance of its proposals. But if these are amended or rejected by Member State Governments the Commission cannot overrule them.

It can refer countries to the European Court for alleged failures to follow EU laws that have already been agreed. But here again the Commission has no votes: it is up to the judges to decide.

Despite popular perception, the Commission has no actual powers to 'govern' Europe and quite right too.

This idea has nonetheless gained currency because so many decisions are now taken at EU level by Qualified Majority Voting (QMV). This is a complicated numerical formula, weighted by size of country, to express the simple concept that if a majority of countries agree to something then the minority will just have to grin and bear it.

The popular view is that the UK does most of the bearing, though without much of the grinning. It is not actually true.

It so often seems that Brussels is telling us what to do, which implies that the UK is being regularly outvoted by the other countries. That must be why we are constantly compelled to accept measures we don't like. The truth is that rightly or wrongly our own Government has agreed almost all these measures in the first place. The UK is regularly siding with the majority – that is to say that the majority is regularly siding with the UK.

France has found itself outvoted on many more occasions. If it wasn't for QMV, France would not have to give in.

This shows why QMV can be such a good idea.

It was the Thatcher Government that agreed to a major extension of QMV way back in 1986 in signing the Single European Act. Maggie realised this was the only way to unlock progress on completing the Single Market. If every country retained the right to block every change, then certain countries would do just that. They would help their own domestic industries and lock out outsiders. An open Common Market would never be delivered.

The only way to drive change was and is for all countries to surrender some individual national vetoes in certain agreed trade areas, and then for all to accept the resultant compromises. Hiding behind "national sovereignty" simply helps protectionism. If real sovereignty is translated as meaning real power, you have to agree some majority voting to secure it.

The danger is that the principle of QMV could in practice all too easily spread to other areas outside trade, to cover taxation, asylum and immigration, a European Public Prosecutor and an EU criminal justice system. If the proposed EU Constitution is agreed, that is exactly what would happen. There must be a limit on how wide QMV goes: Conservatives believe it should focus essentially on trade. That is why this new Commission could actually be a force for good.

Back in 2000, during the six-month Portuguese Presidency, the European Council agreed a memorable action plan. Called the Lisbon Agenda, it pledged to make the EU "the most competitive and dynamic knowledge-based economy in the world by 2010, with more and better jobs and greater social cohesion". It was a splendid vision, though Dutch Commissioner Frits Bolkestein was to declare later that the statement was "all poetry and no motion" since nobody had done anything to make it happen.

The new Commission, led by its new Portuguese President Barroso, is determined to deliver this objective. In so doing it is not trying to impose its own will upon Member State Governments represented in the European Council. It is taking the Council at its word and trying to translate it into action. Barroso has pledged to put competitiveness at the top of his agenda. If this happens, some of the EU red-tape accumulated over the years will have to be rolled back. That would make the Commission the Good Guys.

But meanwhile the Commission is still branded the Bad Guys. It is still regarded as responsible for the stream of EU social legislation increasingly intruding into every nook and cranny of our lives even though, in its defence, it is essentially fulfilling the declared will of Member States.

The Commission is also regarded as being at best incompetent and at worst condoning fraud because the EU auditors are not prepared to sign off the annual accounts, even though most of the fraud is committed within Member States.

In addition, the Commission is constantly castigated for being made up of unelected bureaucrats. True, Commissioners are appointed, and true they are bureaucrats. That is what they are supposed to be. The UK Civil Service also consists of a positive army of unelected bureaucrats (actually many times bigger than the real army) but that never seems to be an issue. Perhaps this is because they are British, so that makes it alright. What they do, however, is not alright at all.

The Head of Tax at Price Waterhouse Coopers has stated that nowadays when advising US Companies where to base their European Headquarters, they seldom recommend the UK "because the UK is not competitive in a whole range of areas".

A survey amongst members of German Industry UK, which represents 230 German firms in the country, pinpointed the problem precisely.

Quoted in the *Sunday Times* in December 2004, GIUK President Dr Bernd Atenstaedt said: "Germany is trying to reduce regulations but Britain is increasing them so the gap is closing. German companies came here because it was easier to operate, but that is changing. It isn't just the

European Union: it is also what the British Government is introducing in terms of new regulations".

The Commission is conveniently blamed for every piece of heavy-handed regulation that the British don't like. Somehow the UK Government never get round to correcting this misconception. It is so much easier to let another take the blame.

Most EU laws are in the form of Directives, which only have legal force once they are transposed into the national laws of Member States via their own national Parliaments. Directives are often relatively short documents when they leave the Commission. They are rather longer when they have gone via our own Civil Servants.

When the Working Time Directive first came out I was running two food manufacturing businesses, in the Black Country and the Netherlands. I wrote to the two Governments asking for advice as to how to implement the directive. The Dutch Government sent me eight pages of guidance notes; these were very straightforward and pretty common-sensical.

The UK Government sent me 134 pages, together with a covering letter saying that these were only interim notes as fuller guidance would become available once various aspects had been clarified in the Courts.

A recent study by the British Chambers of Commerce: 'How much regulation is gold-plate?' contains many rich examples of our own Civil Service at work. The original EU Directive 2002742/EC on the maximum pesticide residues in certain foods consists of 1,167 words in the original text. The UK implementing regulation runs to 27,046 words. Directive 70/157 on the sound level of exhaust systems of motor vehicles was implemented in the UK via 26 separate statutory instruments.

The Country Land & Business Association has also highlighted an EU Directive on the slaughter of calves, where the UK implementing regulation requires farmers to register births of all calves within 27 days or face strict penalties. In Spain the comparable deadline is six months.

This is not gold-plating: it is lead-plating in terms of the extra weight of excessive regulation imposed on UK industry.

Meanwhile Brussels remains the standby scapegoat for all red tape. The Tale of the Bouncy Castles is a lovely example.

In autumn 2004 a local West Midlands paper ran the story that a certain Borough Council had been compelled to create the job of Bouncy Castle Inspector "following an EU Health & Safety Directive." I investigated this personally and have found no such Directive.

There has indeed been discussion going on at EU level about the different national safety standards and test methods for inflatable equipment such as bouncy castles. But this discussion has been solely between the individual national safety standards agencies of the various Member States. Any possible move to agreed standards across the EU would be purely voluntary. It would certainly seem eminently sensible that there should be such EU-wide standards if possible, so that parents could be reassured that bouncing in Barcelona could be as safe as bouncing in Blackpool. But there was to be no need for a formal Directive.

Anyway, all national agencies were comparing notes with a deadline of end November 2004 with no conclusions being reached in the meantime.

But that did not stop the UK Government jumping the gun and issuing its own range of extremely stringent guidelines in advance. It was these that the Borough Council duly decided to follow. If it hadn't, and there had been an accident in any of its Council-run playgrounds, it might have been sued for negligence. Thus did guidelines become rules.

Meanwhile national newspapers such as the *Daily Express* began screaming out headlines such as: 'Now EU puts speed limits on children's roundabouts'. One article went on to highlight a maximum of two swings per bay instead of three in playgrounds, a maximum speed of five metres per second for rotating items, and footrests for rocking equipment where the ground clearance is less than 230 millimetres.

Except this didn't come from Brussels. As so often, it came from the most professional bureaucrats in Europe.

The real *Kommissars* are in Westminster and Whitehall.

CHAPTER 20

Not Enough Rules

Britain is fast becoming submerged by new rules of one kind or another. But there is one area where we don't have enough rules: the twin issues of asylum and immigration control.

Official estimates suggest as many as 500,000 people enter the European Union illegally every year, mainly from the North Africa, Asia and the Balkan states. Between 100,000 and 200,000 successfully make it to Britain, disappearing into the black economy.

It is no surprise that so many people want to come to the UK. We have a proud record in terms of human rights and race relations. We have warmly welcomed the many Ugandan Asians escaping Idi Amin, as well as thousands fleeing persecution from Iraq and Afghanistan. We have a rich variety of happy and successful ethnic communities to which newcomers can bond. We have a National Health Service, effectively free to all-comers. We speak English as our first language. Finally, compared with many EU countries, the UK has relatively generous social welfare benefits.

But all this simply increases the problem. The UK is getting really rather full.

Sir Andrew Green, Chairman of Migrationwatch UK, has observed that while the Netherlands is the most densely crowded EU country overall, the South-East of England is twice as crowded. England now has more people per square mile than the whole of India. And the numbers are still going up.

In 2002 net foreign immigration, i.e. the numbers that arrive officially less those that leave, reached nearly 250,000 people. This was more than double the level of 1997 when Labour came to power. The Government's own figures project an increase in UK population by 5.6 million over the next 30 years – five times the population of Birmingham – and 85% of this increase will be from new immigrants.

At least a quarter of all new houses needed in the next 15 years will be just for them. The strain on public services, especially in smaller communities, is already immense.

Meanwhile, 1.5 million new visas are issued every year to visitors and students, but no checks are made to see if they leave. They may well be still here. Almost one-third of all asylum applicants entering the EU choose the UK to lodge their application, more than any other Member State, presumably in part at least because they see us as a soft touch. 90% have their claims turned down, but only 10% of those rejected are physically deported. The rest just disappear, and must still be here.

The cost of just processing asylum seekers alone reached £3.5billion in total for the two years 2001-2003, virtually the same as our annual membership fee to the European Union. £1billion alone goes on accommodation and financial support: asylum-seekers get housing, food and clothing allowances because while their claims are being processed they are officially banned from working. Although the Immigration Directorate employed nearly 14000 people in 2003-4 compared with 5,400 in 1996, cases can still take years to resolve. The cost of legal aid alone is approaching £250 million.

The fact that many people nowadays are very concerned about asylum and immigration does not make them racist. In fact recent polls suggest that even within existing ethnic communities, already happily settled in the UK, over 50% also want to see much tougher immigration rules. When services have to be rationed and prioritised, as they have to be under any Government, people understandably resent newcomers jumping to the top of the queue.

They resent the political correctness of organisations so keen to avoid offence to the newcomers that they offend those already here. I have happily joined in celebrations of the festivals of Diwali and Eid: but when the Labour-run Birmingham City Council ruled we had to celebrate 'Winterval' instead of Christmas I found this offensive. When the Red Cross removed Christmas Trees from its charity shop windows, claiming – with no evidence – that such a sign of a Christian festival might upset non-Christians, it upset many others. When schools agree the importance of their pupils learning a second language, but suggest it should be Urdu, I consider they have got it very wrong.

We should absolutely encourage our ethnic communities to preserve their own culture and heritage, but not at the expense of the culture and heritage of those already here.

People also resent absence of action from politicians. Time can readily be found for legislation to abolish hunting, but not apparently to address a real problem that looms larger by the day.

And people are not impressed by a Home Secretary who has talked tough, but who will be mainly remembered for other reasons. Specifically it now appears that in a fit of excess zeal his department not only fast-tracked the visa application for his latest lover's nanny, but in the process opened the way for thousands of others to join her in the UK – thereby giving a new meaning to the phrase 'the Nanny State'.

Our country cannot continue to be a free-for-all. We need an active asylum and immigration policy that provides firmer controls and is fairer to existing communities. We need the three major political parties to show leadership and to work together in the common cause. We need less Government spin and more real action. We need it fast.

That is why Michael Howard has proposed a radical plan for a strict annual national quota of immigrants, to be voted on by Parliament. A points system would then select as a priority those with skills, with family ties here or with capital to invest. The whole asylum control process would also be reformed. In his own words, the rules would be designed to "help genuine refugees, and give priority to those who want to come to Britain to work hard and make a positive contribution."

He has also proposed to pull out of the specific 1951 Geneva Convention on refugees. This was designed to cope with the political problems of post-war Europe, not the economic mass migration that is happening today.

These proposals are bold and imaginative. They at last provide a framework of rules that address the issues. Until measures like these are put in place, the answer to the question 'Who rules Britannia?' is very clear.

On this issue, frankly: Nobody.

CHAPTER 21

Counting the Cost

Counting the cost of the UK's membership of the EU has produced some wildly different answers. It all depends on who you ask.

One of the farthest-fetched figures has come from one of the loopier Lords, who reckoned it was as much as £40billion a year. In a pamphlet in autumn 2004 he assembled his arithmetic as follows:

- The Netherlands Finance Minister has apparently computed that over-regulation costs the Dutch 2% of GDP;
- Most regulation comes from the EU;
- UK GDP is £1000billion p.a.
- Therefore the EU must cost the UK 2% of this, or £20billion in extra regulation alone.

On top of that, he somehow assesses a cost of £15.6billion as the UK share of the Common Agricultural Policy, made up of higher prices on food and higher taxes to subsidise farmers.

Finally he includes as well the official net contribution of around £4billion (based on our paying out £11billion each year direct to the EU but then getting about £7billion back).

His creative accounting has carefully converted this £4billion net payment into an annual cost figure of £40billion, a tenfold increase.

All political parties would be screaming for a better deal if there were the remotest reality in these manufactured numbers. The fact that they aren't suggests that there isn't.

The actual £4billion net contribution is indeed the real figure, but even this is worth putting into context.

Since Labour came to power, taxes have risen by nearly £60billion a year.

New Government quangos cost well over £20billion of this. The David James Report has identified as much as £35billion of current Government expenditure as wasted.

Total annual UK Government expenditure is currently a record £450billion. The UK net contribution to the EU is just under 1% of this. Gordon Brown raises this sum in less than a day.

Even this figure is arguably overstated. It is generally accepted (by all EU Member State Governments) that the benefits of increased trade within the EU as a direct result of membership is worth between 1.4% and 1.8% of GDP. Given our net contribution is only around 1%, this means the UK actually makes a profit on trade leaving aside any political benefits.

Meanwhile it should be noted that while the absolute level of the EU budget has increased over the years as Member States' economies have grown, the actual rate of increase over the past seven years has been half the increase of Member States' own budgets. The latter is where the real cost problem lies.

There are of course are lies, damn lies, and statistics. The question is, which are which?

CHAPTER 22

The Great Deception

UKIP supporters should not be derided or dismissed. They care passionately about their country. But they have no monopoly on patriotism: it is our country too.

They want what we should all want, a strong and prosperous country, with freedom to live our own lives within society without being told what to do by bossy bureaucrats and meddling politicians.

We are indeed strong and prosperous, but do not feel free. We feel the noose of the Nanny State tightening daily. But in our eagerness to blame Brussels for all our woes and fears, we forget that Nanny lives in Whitehall and in Westminster. It is there that laws are hatched decreeing how parents may discipline children, how many hours homework must be done, how we cannot fight back burglars within our own home, what food we should eat, where we may smoke, how dangerous it is for kids to play conkers, and which students should be granted places at universities. These are the diktats now ruling Britannia.

It is the current Government that has shredded our Constitution, trying to divide the country into regions, trying to disband the 1,500-year old office of the Lord Chancellor, putting scores of party political spin-doctors onto the Government payroll.

It is the current Government that has decimated our pensions, driven a doubling of Council tax, and raised 66 other taxes to fund the growing battalions of civil servants: more extra civil servants have been employed each year under Tony Blair than are employed by the entire European Commission.

It is the current Prime Minister who has completely sidelined the House of Commons, seldom bothering to turn up even to vote.

Continental EU has its own problems. There, the standard Socialist one-size-fits-all straitjacket has gridlocked countries such as Germany into chronic unemployment. Some rules may be specific to some Member States. But most are conceived in Brussels, and these are the ones supported by the UK Government. The worst are officially opposed by the Government in the European Council, while being actively promoted by Labour MEPs with tacit Government permission in the European Parliament. In both cases, rules affecting Britannia are being shaped and endorsed by British Labour politicians who then deny any responsibility.

UKIP maintains that Brussels Rules Britannia, that there is

nothing we can do from within, that we would be freer as well as better off if we left. None of this is true.

The real deception is the basic UKIP message.

It is a deception to maintain that all mainstream political parties are the same. Only the Conservatives have been the consistent champions of choice. Only Conservatives have been fighting to keep the Pound and resisting the European Constitution while at the same time leading the campaign to complete the Single Market.

It is a deception to claim that our link with the EPP political Group is a betrayal of our manifesto and a denial of our faith. Conservatives are crystal clear that the main threat to the future of Europe, and of our own country, comes from allowing the shackles of Socialism to bind us tight. We know our enemy, and we know the old adage is very true: he who is not my friend is my enemy.

We also know the converse is also true: he who shares the same enemy must be my friend. Partnership with such friends is the only way to win. Any other course – every other course – simply aids the other side.

It is a deception to declare that the UK can make no difference to what happens in the EU, because everything has allegedly already been pre-ordained. We do not have to sign up to the Single Currency: John Major negotiated a UK opt-out. We did not have to sign up to the Social Chapter: John Major got an opt-out there too, though this was soon to be wantonly tossed aside by Tony Blair. We don't have to sign up to the proposed EU Constitution, thanks to the Conservative campaign to let the people decide. We pay far less nowadays for membership than we did at the outset because Margaret Thatcher secured a rebate currently worth £4 billion a year. Indeed it should be worth progressively more every year from now, unless Blair gives this away too.

It is a deception to imply we have no friends in Europe, that the UK is always isolated. When Britain wishes to make a stand on legislative issues, there are plenty of partners ready to stand with us. There are many countries, especially those from 'New Europe', that share the Conservative vision of a looser, more flexible EU. They are most willing to stand together alongside: their disappointment is that the current UK Government so seldom makes any stand.

It is a deception to state that if we detached from the EU we would thereby re-attach more sovereignty to ourselves. In this world of globalisation, of political power as well as trade, the four future powerhouses of China, India, the EU and the USA will take the big decisions. We can be an active part of that process, using shared sovereignty to influence events. Or we can proudly lay claim to independent sovereignty, while watching it ebb away as others decide.

Real sovereignty is the practical power to shape events in one's own interest. In theory King Canute had absolute power as sovereign: in practice he could not roll back the tide.

It is a deception to promise that if we left we could still trade freely with our current EU partners. We would still be bound by rules we could not shape, and by tariffs or quotas we would have to observe. Indeed without Conservative pressure on the inside many non-tariff barriers would remain more firmly in place. The UK would be doubly disadvantaged.

It is a deception to claim that UK jobs would be unaffected if we left. Multi-national companies who use us as a gateway into Europe would go straight out of the door.

It is a deception that EU withdrawal would unlock funds for the UK to spend on building more hospitals and schools. £9billion is already wasted every year from the UK Health budget alone. Conservatives have identified over £35billion of Labour waste that could be either lopped off all our tax bills or go into real improvements in public services. Our net membership contribution to the EU budget is small in comparison, and in any event we would still have to pay a hefty fee in order to trade just as Norway does.

It is a deception to claim that a protest vote will somehow convince the Conservative Party to vote for the political and economic cul-de-sac of withdrawal. Conservatives would never agree to make our country weaker.

It is also a deception to maintain that a protest vote is damage-free, when it simply promotes a clearer run for the two main federalist parties in local, national and European elections alike.

Finally it is positively daft to single out the Conservatives as the main target of such a protest. The real protest should be against a Government that is letting Britain down in so many ways.

It is Labour that is failing to fight our corner in Europe. It is Labour that believes that the State should spend more of our money, and place more restrictions on how we spend our lives. It is Labour that is the real threat to those democratic freedoms that used to be nurtured within our beloved country.

For those who care about who rules Britannia, the answer is not to say goodbye to the EU.

It is to say goodbye to Tony, to Gordon, and to Charles.